To David Hathaway

I know it's not what you had in mind, but it's a start.

And to my husband, Neil

For your excitement, support and encouragement.

Cover design by

Tamberlee King

Cover photo by

Derek Armstrong

Pickles

The

Parrot

Georgi Abbott

Chapter One

Georgi Gets a Parrot

What the hell have I done?

Our new African Grey Congo Parrot, Pickles, has just settled in his new cage in our living room. He went in willingly enough and I quickly closed the cage door and fell in a heap on the couch. I lay there staring at him, and he at me. Silence, while we each pondered our new living situations.

A couple of days ago, I had contacted some parrot breeders (Thomas & Sylvia) who had a lone African Grey, one in a clutch and three months old. Knowing Pickles, having lived with and being possessed by him for eight years, I now suspect he killed and ate his siblings. All attention, at all times, must be solely directed toward him. Having siblings would only cramp his style.

My husband Neil and I live in the interior of British Columbia, Canada. Thomas and Sylvia live on Vancouver Island. No quick trip. 4 hours drive to the ferry, a couple of hours early to ensure passage and a two-hour ferry ride. My mother, Zoe, lives on the coast so I over-nighted with her and she accompanied me on the ocean voyage. Mom didn't say much when I told her I was getting a parrot but I don't think she understood the attraction.

Thomas and Sylvia met us on the other side, at the ferry terminal. It was very much like a drug deal, or even a kidnapping, as we were ushered from the arrival area and hustled into the side doors of a van. They looked nice enough, but they always say that during a television interview about the neighbor who was just arrested for murdering, dismembering and burying a body in his back yard.

Once in the van, the exchange began. Pickles, who had not been named yet, was removed from a small cage. He 'stepped up' readily and after admiring him briefly, he was handed off to me. I had to impress these people for the deal to be approved so I swallowed my fear of strong beaks and reached for him. I had owned budgies and cockatiels and was under the impression that you put your finger firmly on the bottom of the chest to coerce a bird to step up. In all my parrot research since then, I have discovered that's wrong, not to mention annoying for the bird. They must have thought I was nuts but everything went smoothly as I chatted with Pickles, fed him some mash, wiped his beak and even got some kisses. Having retained my lips, I was thrilled with my little package.

A rolled up wad of cash was exchanged and mom and I boarded the return ferry. Pickles had been inserted in a plastic dog kennel with built-in perch and covered up. I had been warned that fumes from the car deck could be toxic to Pickles so he was smuggled to the upper decks. I didn't do a very good smuggling job since I couldn't resist lifting the blanket to interact with Pickles – a lot. Mom was taking a shine to him too, lifting the blanket often to chat with him. He attracted much attention from other ferry passengers and he was pretty cool with that. He mostly cooed, chirped and whistled with the odd grating little screech sound, which over the next couple of days, I learned did not reflect a happy mood.

I over-nighted at moms again and some other family members came to see the parrot. Pickles was enjoying the attention and all the food treats but soon tired. By now, he had grown to resent his small accommodations so getting him in the kennel became more and more difficult. He'd just latch on to my finger and

2

refuse to step down on the perch. I finally got him bedded and covered for the night then we arose early to beat the heat for the four-hour drive home.

Pickles had had enough driving. Very quickly, he latched himself to the holes in the sides of the kennel with his beak and talons and began his insistent little screech. I felt bad but my God! How long can one endure that sound? Pickles was irritated, I was getting cranky as hell and the second-guessing of myself began. It was hot and I had to be careful about opening windows because I had read that parrots could die in drafts. What the heck is a draft?? Any moving air at all? Just cold air? I wasn't sure and I wasn't taking any chances so windows remained closed. We both got crankier and crankier until I was sure Pickles had stopped liking me, and I didn't give a damn because I was ready to ring his little neck.

But we endured, we were home and now we sat staring at each other. The last couple of days had been such a whirlwind, everything happened so fast. I mean, I had just been *thinking* of getting a parrot. I didn't think I would find one so quickly and all the research I had done the past year did not prepare me. I was getting an anxiety attack. Along with my exhaustion, panic set in, followed by depression. I lay down on the couch and before I fell into a deep sleep, I drifted off thinking about my first bird, a blue budgie named Cheery.

My parents presented me with Cheery when I was a young girl. He was a beautiful little blue bird, both friendly and mischievous. He liked to give little kisses and nibble on an ear or play with my hair. His favorite thing was on family birthdays or other occasions when cards were displayed on the TV, he would drag them all to the edge and watch them float to the floor. He was allowed to fly free in the house a lot and I remember him landing smack dab in the middle of a lemon meringue pie my mom had baked. He wasn't happy about this at all and he let us know by giving us the evil eye and angry chirps between cleaning sticky pie off his feathers.

3

He talked a lot for a little budgie. He knew all the names of our family of 6 and a few phrases. One year I taught him to sing "Here Comes Santa Clause" and "Grouchy Mr. Clemens" to the tune of "Ring Around the Rosie". Mr. Clemens was my dad and I thought it would be funny for my dad to hear that one day. And it was. I'll never forget the look on my dad's face the first time he heard it. Cheery would sometimes get confused and start to sing the Santa song but end up with my dad's song, resulting in "Here Comes Grouchy Mr. Clemens".

Cheery was a great little guy and the beginning of my love for birds of any kind. He flew out the door one day when someone wasn't paying attention and even though we put ads in every paper, laundry mat and store, we never saw him again. I had several budgies after that and at one point, a cockatiel but my whole life, I dreamt of having a parrot.

I grew up with dogs, cats, birds, pet mice – anything I could talk my parents into letting me have. I had a fascination with frogs, toads, snakes and bugs and would sometimes collect them and keep them in my room, much to my mother's horror. She found worms in my pockets when she did my laundry, jars of slugs when she cleaned my room and it seemed I was always shoving something in her face telling her to "Look Mom!"

She didn't mind my pet toad but she talked me into releasing it in the yard. He turned out to be quite friendly and would greet us if we walked down the path or he would play with our black Lab to pass the time. He hibernated each winter and appeared again each spring until the neighbors removed a pile of boulders along the fence line, where we figured he hibernated, and he never returned the next year.

My white mouse died the day after I took him, against my mother's warnings, for a bicycle ride. I had him in my handlebar carriage and mom told me the weather

4

was too cold for him and that he'd get sick. The next morning I found him dead in his cage. I was devastated and sick with guilt but mom wouldn't let me stay home from school for a day of mourning. At lunchtime, I talked my friend Bonnie into coming home with me so we could have a proper funeral so we packed him in a shoebox and buried him beneath my bedroom window. When the neighbor lady saw us and realized what we were up to, she told us to go back to school. It's only a mouse, she said. I always liked this lady but that day I thought she was a cruel old broad. A few months later, my curiosity got the best of me and I dug up the grave but there was nothing left to find.

I would spend hours watching a spider catch and wrap a fly in his web and I can remember watching maggots slowly devour a dead cat every day on my way home from school. Birds and their nests were especially interesting to me but my mom kept me away from baby birds by telling me that once my scent was on a baby or the nest, the mother would reject or kill the bird. I was fascinated with anything live. And now, I had a real live parrot.

Hours later, I awoke. What a good bird, he hadn't made a sound while I slept. He didn't then, and he doesn't to this day. This is a blessing as we like to nap on our couches, and well, there is the odd hangover day. Even in the mornings, Pickles remains under cover while singing and chatting to himself until we get up. The only time he ever demands out is if we completely forget about him. Why, what a quiet, considerate bird! This isn't toooooo bad, I thought.

Neil arrived home from the fly shop, which we owned and operated at the time, and I introduced man and bird. Pickles liked him right off the bat but we soon found out that Pickles likes everybody right off the bat. Neil was a little hesitant about touching him but quickly found that Pickles readily welcomed scratches and kisses.

Then there were the cats. Three of them. Thomas had assured me that Pickles wouldn't be afraid of cats, as he had spent his first 3 months with small dogs. This turned out to be true but we had concerns about the cats being too interested in him. They were at first. The interest quickly turned to fear the first time Pickles displayed his wingspan. We never had a problem between the cats and parrot but by the end of Pickles first year with us, all 3 cats had disappeared. Probably owls, but again, I suspect Pickles eliminated them. An empty lap meant available hands for perching.

We pondered names but I basically dismissed any of Neil's suggestions except for Logan. Eventually we settled on Pickles. When I was a little girl, the old man down the lane nicknamed me that because I liked dill pickles. It seemed a perfect fit for our new bird.

Things were awkward at times with Pickles that first night. We were unsure of how to entertain him and just holding him on our hands grew a little boring after awhile, for him and for us. I still doubted my decision to get a parrot but the next day removed all my doubts once and for all. I had been overtired from the long, stressful trip and it had clouded my judgment. Come to think of it, every pet I ever owned caused me to have a panic attack the first day I brought them home.

Upon waking, I jumped out of bed and ran to the living room to remove the cage cover. I was greeted with the sweetest little face, a cluck and a coo, and I fell in love right there and then. As I opened the door and locked it into place so that it wouldn't swing shut on Pickles' little footsies, Pickles scrambled out and propped himself on the top of the door. His head bowed and his neck feathers ruffled, signaling he wanted a scratch. He stepped up readily and we went to the couch to get better acquainted.

It was immediately apparent that Pickles was bursting with personality and character. He had adapted to his new home with no apparent signs of stress and

6

little or no fear with new objects, sounds or movements. Pickles has never become much of a cuddling bird, preferring to sit on a knee, hand or couch arm but he definitely has his moments. Right from the start, you just knew he was a confident, well-adjusted bird who could turn on the charm with the flick of a switch. He was smart – too damn smart, with a little streak of pure evil. A deadly combination.

Right off the bat, Pickles preferred his human interaction to be straightforward and sensible. Just sit and chat with some playing thrown in, such as swinging on a towel, throwing a towel over him, playing tickle, tickle (as Pickles would say - ticko, ticko) or having my fingers chase after him to "grab his little chicken toes".

He wasn't particularly destructive although for a few years, buttons were snapped off in a blink of an eye and all clothing was pocked with little beak holes. TV remotes were completely fascinating and there was no obstacle that could keep him from them.

He knew right away that our laughter was a good thing and he was like a toddler, doing whatever it took to keep it coming. If he ever got in trouble, he'd quickly throw in an antic for distraction. And it usually worked.

I think his first comedic antic was the time he spotted an empty pop bottle that had fallen to the floor. He was down from his cage in a flash and running toward it before we had a chance to pick it up. When he got to it, he lowered his head like a bull before a charge and stood there clucking at it. When the bottle didn't respond, he gave it a quick shove, which sent the bottle rolling and Pickles took up the chase. A few shoves and rolls later, Pickles decided to hop on it and suddenly found himself doing the barrel roll with wings aflapping, ending in a face plant on the carpet.

The bottle needed to be taught a lesson so he grabbed it by the neck with his talon and waved it in the air with a loud verbal assault. He alternated between waving it in the air and smashing it on the floor until he misjudged and bonked himself in the head. This made him angrier and he waved it harder, until he got bonked again! The angrier he got, the more spastic his motions so he just kept getting bonked. Finally, he tossed it away and as he turned to leave, the bottle came after him – a result of its ricochet off the table. Pickles ran screaming to my feet, scrambled up my leg and sat there all fluffed up while muttering as he glanced angrily over his shoulder to make sure the bottle wasn't following.

Since Pickles was happiest sitting on a lap or couch arm, he quickly realized that talking was in his best interest. He knew a few words before we got him but now he spat out new words at staple gun speed and used them wisely. We've never really taught Pickles words, we merely converse with him as you would a young child learning to speak and connect meanings to words, for the most part.

Pickles was cheeky and sneaky and full of sass. Teasing and torturing were his past time, everybody and everything was fair game. The first real proof we got was the day he was sitting on the top perch of his cage, digging in to his hanging bucket of talon toys and tossing them with pinpoint accuracy into his water dish below. Once the bucket was empty and the water bowl full, he toodled down to sit on the side of the bowl to pick out the toys, one by one, and throw them to the cage floor.

The small white whiffle ball, filled with pony beads, was saved until last. This poor toy was destined for torture. He eyed it softly, purring to it as he gently plucked it from the water with his talon "Hello baby. Step up. Good boy!" he praised. He caressed it lovingly against his ears, clucking and cooing and then, having successfully seduced the ball into submission, he turned on it....

He waved it savagely in the air, held it next to his beak and began the interrogation. "Want some fresh water? HUH? WANT SOME FRESH WATER?" he demanded. Before the ball could get its bearings and answer, it was quickly submerged and held beneath the water.

Just as the poor little ball was on the verge of drowning, he yanked it out and waved it violently in the air shouting "WANT SOME FRESH WATER? HUH?" but before the little ball could answer, it was quickly dunked again. This went on several times until Pickles cast the choking, sputtering ball off into the corner in repulsion.

He dismissed the poor defeated ball, climbed out of his cage and turned on *me*. "Wanna grape? Wanna grape! WANNA GRAPE!!" I quickly brought him his grape but he was so embroiled in his tirade that it took him a moment to notice that I'd already set the grape on top of his cage. He shouted on, "WANNA GRAPE! WANNA GRAPE! WANNA GRAPE! WANNA ooooooooo … uh … huuuuuuh." He set upon it and left me in peace, thankful that I had escaped his water torture.

Another time, I handed him a pinecone to chew on, he flung it in my face and told me to "Stop being a brat."

I sang him a song and he spat "Just stop it!"

I was on my hands and knees cleaning up the mess around his cage and he hollered "Get back up!"

I give him a tasty snack and he demands "Want ANOTHER snack."

I leave the room to fetch a different snack and he hollers after me "Be right back!"

I return and give him a grape. He grabs it in his beak, flings it across the room and says, "Want juice."

I give up, sit on the couch and ignore him and he asks politely "Whassa matter? Don't you wanna grape?"

"No" I say, "YOU'RE a brat."

"Bugger" he retorts.

You can't win with him and he always gets the last word. We are emotionally abused parronts and there is no help program available for people like us. We are doomed for life.

I had never heard an African grey scream before and the first time I heard Pickles scream, I almost had a coronary. I came running into the room expecting the worst and found him hanging upside down on a toy. "What's wrong??" I asked, "Are you okay??" He just looked at me and said "Huh?" I stood and watched him for a minute and he just hung there, jabbing at his toys. I figured it was a false alarm and left the room. Immediately he let out a bloodcurdling scream and I ran back to him. He was upside down, flailing his wings and screaming bloody murder. I figured he must have got his toes stuck in the toy so I started to reach for him saying, "It's okay, it's okay. I'll help you." And he went limp, looked at me upside down and said, "Huh?" He was obviously fine, just a little put out that I kept disturbing his play, but I'd had the scare of my life and my first Grey scream experience.

We were struggling to find foods that Pickles liked, he seemed to turn up his nose at most things so it was frustrating to us and we were afraid he wasn't getting enough nutrition. We had read that Greys are social eaters and had even read where people allowed their parrots to dine with them, so we tried it a couple of times. What fools we were. After making our dinner, we placed food on 3 plates – two large for us and one small one for Pickles. Pickles was set on the kitchen table, next to his plate and everybody ate nicely, for about 10 seconds. Suddenly, our food was more appealing to him than his own, even though it was the same food. We thought, okay, let him eat from our plates but then he insisted on stomping straight into the middle of the pile. Now, we're not particularly fussy about feet in our food but all the food on Pickles feet became abstract artwork on every square inch of the table. Our food was only temporarily interesting though, as knives and forks became more important and then glasses, salt and pepper shakers, sugar bowl, napkins and anything else he could pick up or knock over. Dinner became a battle with a dashing, skirting little bundle of feathers. That idea lasted 2 days.

We wondered if just eating in the same room might help. Since Pickles cage was in the living room, we took to eating at the coffee table. We always fed Pickles while we were preparing our own dinner and he would basically ignore his. But as soon as we plopped down our plates and commenced to eat, he couldn't scramble fast enough to his food dish. He ate the entire time we did and didn't stop until we finished. Case solved!

Pickles prefers routine but he's not as fanatic about it as some African Greys. He's content waiting for people to rise in the morning, he just sits and chats to himself. However, breakfast has to follow pretty darn quickly after the cover comes off. For the first few minutes he constantly greets us with "Good morning!" but soon turns to "Want breakfast." Back then, I had my computer in the kitchen (I've since moved it into the guest room) and Pickles' cage was situated next to a window divider in the living room, which looks in to the kitchen. While Pickles eats his breakfast, I check emails and attend to work related things. One morning, on garbage day, I dragged myself out of bed and put the water on for coffee. I lugged the garbage cans through the snow, plunked them at the end of the driveway and placed heavy rocks on top so the crows couldn't flip the lids.

11

With frozen hands, I fed Pickles then sat down at the computer to drink my coffee and warm up.

Not 5 minutes later, I hear a sound. A chattering kind of sound. I stop and listen – it stops. I go back to reading emails and there it goes again. I glance through the window between the kitchen and the living room and Pickles is sitting on his perch, next to the window, all fluffed up and half asleep so it can't be him.

I go back to my emails and the chattering starts again. I look at Pickles but he's just sitting there, still half asleep. Then it hits me, that's the sound of a squirrel! Shoot, it must have snuck through the open door while I was taking the garbage out. The sound seems to be coming from the living room so I go and investigate but don't see anything. I check the mudroom, can't see anything there either.

Back to the computer, take a sip of coffee and there's the sound again. This time I'm sure it's coming from the living room so I tear the place apart. Nope. Nothing. Hmmm.

This time, I go back to the computer, put my elbow on the desk, cradle my forehead in my hands and pretend to be looking at the computer while I'm actually peeking through my fingers at Pickles. It's not long before I hear the chattering and see Pickles' open beak and vibrating throat.

"Aha!! I say. "It was you all along!"

"Goof" he mumbles as he closes his eyes to sleep.

Pickles learned to say "Wanna snack" very quickly. That, and "Poop on the paper." We use pine nuts for training and rewards. They are very expensive but he loves them more than anything. In the beginning, I would have him sit on my knee and ask him "Wanna snack?" and then give him one. I think it took about a

12

day before he asked for one and the minute he did, I handed it to him. I think he was in shock. He had asked for one, and one appeared! He was taken aback for a minute but then ate it and right away and asked for another one. I was thrilled that he learned so quickly but from then on, he drove us crazy asking for them.

Soon, after asking for a snack and being rewarded with one, I'd ask him if he wanted another snack. It was uncanny the way he picked that up. He always asked first "Wanna snack?" and the next time was "Wanna nudder snack?" He has never asked for 'another snack' before asking for the first one.

He has picked up on the difference between asking for something and stating that he wants something. For example, if he wants a snack but isn't sure if we'll give him one, he'll ask for it (?) but if he really wants it and maybe we're not listening, or refuse to give him one, he will demand "Wanna snack!"

He has since applied this to many things. If everyone is home, he will state "Everybody's home! Woo hoo!" but if we are in another room and he can't see us, he asks "Anybody home?" If he's in a good mood, he will sweetly ask, "Wanna go for a walk?" but if he's bored and cranky, he says, "Wanna go for a walk!!"

We taught him early on to poop on paper below his play stands. We put paper below the front 2 corners where he liked to sit on the bottom of his play stand to protect the carpet. Then, every time he'd poop there, we'd tell him "Good boy! Poop on the paper!" and hand him a snack. It didn't take long before he'd sit there and ask for a snack and we'd tell him "Poop on the paper. Poop for a snack." And he would. Sometimes, he'd be so busy pooping for snacks, he'd be fresh out of poop but he'd try. He'd shake and shake his bottom and strain to get one out but there was nothing except a little "phfft" sound. They say birds don't fart but I'm telling you, he managed to get air.

If we noticed Pickles on the top branches of his play stand, preparing to take a poop, we would say, "No, no, no, poop on the paper for a snack" and after a few days of coaxing, he would come down to the corner to do his business. Often, he would be playing on the top branches of his play stand and suddenly stop and go "No, no, no, no, no, no … poop … no, no, no, no, no … poop on the paper." then climb, fast as hell, down to the right spot, take his poop and say, "Good boy! Poop on the paper for a snack!"

He's always had a bit of a fascination with his poop. He likes to let it loose and cock his head to watch it fall. He'll stare at his artwork and remark, "mmmmmm".

Pickles is camera shy, always has been. I don't know why but from the first time we ever pulled the camera out, he'd run and hide behind something or he'd go from sitting all fluffed up and cute as a button, to stretching and sleeking himself out toward the camera. We always end up with this big head in the foreground, skinny body behind and Pickles with a look on his face as if to say, "Get that damn thing OUT of my FACE!"

Videos are hard to take too. If I want a video of Pickles, I have to place it somewhere and leave the room. The trouble with that is, Pickles moves around and ends up out of the line of the camera. I have a couple of videos with Pickles chatting himself up but I'd like to get some film of us interacting and talking with him too.

Pickles likes to go for swings on a hand towel. I hold it above him and he grabs on to the bottom and pushes off as I swing the towel back and forth with him hanging upside down. "Shwing baby shwing!" he goes. "Woo hoo!" he exclaims. Suddenly he's climbing the towel towards my hand and there's no way I want that. Pickles gets rough with his beak when playing and I don't want him to latch on to a finger so just as he reaches the top, I grab the bottom of the towel with the other

14

hand and flip the towel so he's back down on the bottom. He figures, this is fun and scampers back up.

This game takes dexterity. If your timing is off, you're going to wind up with a bird hanging by the beak from a finger. At one point, in my haste to flip the towel, I let go of one end before I had a hold of the other. Pickles fell and landed perfectly in a little rectangular box I had left on the couch, with the towel crumpling on top of him. I lifted the towel to find him tightly wedged on his back, snug as a glove. He was not happy and his feet were flailing in the air as he growled his displeasure. "Step up!" he demanded. I gave him my finger to grasp and raised him up but the box came with him. I couldn't resist … I flipped them both around so Pickles was on his feet, wearing the box on his back. He had no idea what to do and stood still as a statue. Slowly, he took a few steps and started to trot across the cushions but all I could see was a spastic little box, zig zagging across the couch.

I finally rescued him and he proceeded to attack the culprit. He looked like a cobra with wings splayed and neck elongated as he struck the box with his beak in quick, short spurts. He grabbed it and threw it across the couch, went after it and tossed it again and it landed on his head. Bird and box tumbled across the cushions until Pickles emerged the victor and tossed it, once and for all, to the floor.

There's one thing that Pickles picked up almost as soon as we got him. In the mornings, Neil always gets up before me, feeds Pickles, makes my coffee and sets it next to the computer in the kitchen and yells "Cawwwwfeeeee. Come and get your CAAAwwwfeeeee." Or, if I'm ready to get up earlier than he expects, I yell from my bed, "Cawwwwfee" and he gets it ready for me. I don't deserve that man.

One morning, I heard the usual singsong call for coffee so I got up, went to the washroom then sat myself down at the computer and reached for my coffee. But there is no coffee. What the heck? Then I hear "Good morning!" and I look through the window between the kitchen and living room and there's Pickles, hanging on the cage bars with one talon and waving at me with the other. "Want out. Want some breakfast". I look past the cage and there's Neil, sound asleep on the couch. It had been Pickles calling"Cawwwfeeee" in Neil's voice. Not only had he called me for coffee but he'd also made the tinkling sound of the stirring spoon.

Pickles has fooled Neil too. If Neil's in another room, Pickles will call out as if it's me in bed, calling for coffee. He does it quietly, as if it's coming from down the hall and behind the bedroom door. I don't know how many times Neil has opened the bedroom door and told me my coffee's getting cold when I was still sound asleep.

Pickles had become a constant source of entertainment and a wonderful companion. We seldom kept him caged, preferring to interact with him most of the day. His wonderful sense of humor always left you wanting more and we were happy to include him in all family activities.

Chapter 2

Pickles Goes to Work

Right from the beginning, Pickles accompanied us to the fly shop most days. It had always been the plan to have him there with us because we worked almost every day and since Pickles seemed to have settled in quite nicely, we felt a change of scenery would be fine for him. As it turned out, Pickles was in his glory. Since he loved people, he seldom bored of all the interaction from customers. It was obviously the reason he learned to talk so quickly – the more he talked, the more he could abuse everyone who walked in the door.

Within the first few days of being at the shop, he started making the sound of the phone ringing and answering with "Logan Lake Fly Shop."

In the beginning, Pickles was placed on a wooden cross made of branches, which were held up with a Christmas tree stand. It was soon apparent that this just wouldn't do. He was bored and constantly sliding down to the floor where he could be easily trampled by customers, or us. In the next few months, there were a series of set-ups for him until we settled on a cage surrounded by branches that were drilled into the walls. This gave him a play station with lots of hanging toys and the cage was where he went to sleep or eat. He was never locked in the cage unless we had to leave briefly for lunch or supplies. Pickles was usually clipped and seldom flew except a little when he was startled and even then, he basically dropped like a rock.

Within a few weeks, Pickles had developed quite the talking ability. Within months, that ability exploded. He knew that the more he spoke, the more attention he got. He was shooting for the center of the universe.

While owning and operating a fly shop, a large part of our job was to provide fishing reports and suggestions on what type of flies are most effective at the time. There are literally thousands of different variations and names of flies but the only one Pickles learned during all the time he spent in the shop, was the "Woolly Bugger". A popular fly and spoken a lot in the store so Pickles picked up on it up right away, obviously thinking what a cool sound. Perfectly understandable. All the other popular flies were boring words such as Mayflies, Damsels, Dragonflies etc.

At first, he only liked the 'bugger' part of the name so it was inserted into everything, such as Hello bugger, it's raining like a bugger, poop on the bugger, daddy bugger, eat your bugger supper, knick-knack patty whack give a dog a bugger."

Finally he started saying the whole name and when customers jokingly ask, "What's working Pickles?" they were rewarded with the answer, "Woolly Bugger!"

The last guy, after being completely floored by an intelligent response to his question, proceeded to grab a handful of Woolly Buggers from the bin and dump them on the counter. As he was reaching in his wallet to pay for them, he suddenly looked at Pickles, then at me and remarked, "I can't believe I'm actually taking fishing advice from a BIRD." But even more astonishing was that the guy came back 2 days later, floating 2 feet off the ground in excitement and announced that he'd just had the BEST fishing EVER!

There's a good joke that fits Pickles to a tee and it goes like this …

(A lady was walking down the street to work and she saw a parrot on a perch in front of a pet store.

The parrot said to her, "Hey lady, you are really ugly." Well, the lady is furious!

She stormed past the store to her work.

On the way home she saw the same parrot and it said to her, "Hey lady, you are really ugly." She was incredibly ticked now.

The next day the same parrot again said to her, "Hey lady, you are really ugly."

The lady was so ticked that she went into the store and said that she would sue the store and kill the bird. The store manager apologized profusely and promised he would make sure the parrot didn't say it again.

When the lady walked past the store that day after work the parrot called to her, "Hey lady."

She paused and said," Yes?"

The bird said, "You know.")

Pickles has the same snide attitude. A group of 4 guys were bantering back and forth withPickles as they were shopping. Suddenly Pickles got quiet, climbed to his highest perch on the play stand, surveyed the room then demanded "Everybody go home!" Everyone laughed and ignored his command so he barked, "Let's go, let's go, let's go!"

Pickles asked another customer "Wanna sing a song?" so the lady politely obliged with the song "Rockin' Robin" to which Pickles snapped "Wanna GOOD song!"

Then there was the guy who kept nagging Pickles to talk while he was busy preening with his back to us. Finally, he stopped preening long enough to peer over his shoulder and tell the guy to "Go poop on a bug".

We tried and tried to get pickles to say, "How's the fishing?" a polite greeting when people walked in the door but, no way. He liked to greet people with "Hello bugger!" and when they left, it was, "Bye bye. Be gone bugger."

Instead of asking people if they want to buy a fly, it was "Wanna buy a bean? Huh? HUH?"

Now and then, Pickles would get cranky. Slow days were unacceptable and he would start in on me …

Pickles: Wanna go home?

Me: Not yet Pickles.

Pickles: Step up, let's go home.

20

Me: Pretty soon.

Pickles: Let's go home and get some supper. Doncha want some supper?

Me: I'm not hungry.

Pickles: Arncha hungry?

Me: We're NOT going HOME Pickles!

Pickles: Brat.

A parrot in the fly shop turned out to be good for business. Tourists and fly fishermen from around the globe had heard about Pickles and usually made a point of dropping by. At times it was frustrating though. People sometimes hung around a little too much and often they would want to teach him new words or sounds, which we didn't want him copying. Children would hang around too long, taking up room at the counter or keeping us from getting work done. We had to watch them like hawks for fear that items would go missing.

One couple dropped by and while they were shopping around, their 2 kids aged about 3 and 5 tore around the shop, screeching their little heads off. Suddenly, I was hearing it in stereo – the kids on one side of the counter, Pickles on the other. After awhile, the mother came up to pay for her items and while we were making the transaction, she kept cringing at Pickles' screeches. "Doesn't that bird drive you crazy with those sounds?" she asked. I replied, "Do your kids drive you crazy with the sounds *they* make?" She looked offended and said "Of course not." I informed her that Pickles was merely mimicking the sounds that her children had been making for the last 20 minutes and that I would be stuck with those sounds for months. Indeed, 7 years later and he still makes those sounds now and then.

Most people didn't know what kind of bird Pickles was. Once, a lady leaned on the counter staring at him and said "Soooo, what's with the pigeon?" Pickles was often mistaken for a pigeon. Usually, I was happy to answer questions about Pickles and parrots in general but I was getting a little tired of the same old questions, day in and day out.

We were usually pretty busy in the shop but there were some down times, especially during winter. I was making most of Pickles toys by now and often assembled them in the shop during slow periods. People started noticing and soon I was getting requests to make toys for their birds. Before long, I had a little side business going and a window display of bird toys for sale. I was making a small income from it but it became time consuming and I wasn't enjoying it anymore. It was around this time that Hurricane Katrina hit New Orleans and somebody posted on a bird forum about all the lost and homeless parrots. Rescue centres were begging for food and toys so I packed up almost all the toys I had and shipped them down there. Since then, I still make toys but only for Pickles and I'm back to enjoying it.

All in all, Pickles was great company at work and he was happy to entertain both us and our customers. It worked out well and Pickles didn't need to be left home alone all day, every day. He'd get a little needy for attention on slow days and demand to "Go for a walk". So we'd pick him up, carry him around the shop for a while then set him on top of a long display case in the window where he could holler at people outside. Later on, after learning how to bark, he would run back and forth barking at anyone who passed. It was amusing to watch the double takes from people who glanced in, expecting to see a dog. But all in all, he was content to sit quietly and nap or preen when the shop was empty.

One time, Pickles was startled off his play station when someone banged on the wall in the store next to us. Now, Pickles didn't realize that his flight feathers have grown in enough for him to fly at will and after being startled, he took off

22

like a shot, banking and turning like a pro. I think he was as shocked as I that he could be so air borne.

His flight started off well, he soared all the way to the other end of the shop, veering through the curved aisle way and around the clothes rack, disappearing from my sight.

"Pickles?" I called, "Where are you?' No answer. "Pickles?" I call again. I hear a very strained little voice from yonder saying "Huh?" Then silence. I go searching for him and finally I hear a very quiet "Anybody home?" Good, his answer narrows the search down a bit.

I get to the end of the shop and can't see him anywhere; I figure he would have landed on the floor somewhere so I'm looking under the racks and shelving. As I stand there, completely baffled and parrotless, I hear "Hello?" right next to my ear. I turn and there's the little goof, hanging on a peg amidst the dubbing materials on the wall. He's suspended upside down, with his little red twinker up in the air. "Well, this is a fine pickle you've gotten yourself into there Mr. Pickles. Need help?" I ask. As he hung there like a bat, he replied meekly "Give a dog a bone." The old saying immediately came to me, something like "throw a poor guy a bone"; as in help the poor guy out.

So I did. And as I was righting his majesty up, I couldn't help but notice the grey fly tying material he had landed on and realized that Pickles' feathers would make a great substitute! Not long after that, we developed a great fly with his molted feathers and down and dubbed it the Pickle Fly. It caught fish and it was in demand but unfortunately, there was a limit to how many we could tie up as Pickles could only drop a limited amount of feathers.

One day, he climbed down from his play stand at the shop and I was about to pick him up but decided what the heck, let's see what he'll do. He trotted around the counter, straight down the first aisle and made a beeline for the fishing nets. He climbed up the handle of one leaning against the wall and promptly jumped into the net part. Not a smart move. Anyone who's ever tried to walk on a rope net knows this is difficult. In the end, I had to pick the net up by the handle with Pickles tangled in the mesh and try to unravel his feet. His struggles made it worse so I laid the net on the floor to free him.

None the worse for wear, Pickles proceeded to explore from this new, low perspective while I followed, making sure there were no flies and hooks that had dropped on the floor. His trek took him out the open back door and into the lobby of the hotel where somebody was checking in with a dog on a leash. What proceeded was a gentle black lab doing circles around his owner as Pickles scampered after him asking for a kiss. I picked up Pickles and set him in a potted tree in the sitting area while I seated myself on a chair. As people came and went, Pickles called "Hello" and, of course, nobody saw him so they returned the greetings to me. Pickles decided to head down to the dirt so that was the end of his little excursion.

He scared the hell out of me one day. He had been in a frisky, talkative mood but suddenly he went quiet. I turned to look at him and he was upside down, stuck in one of the empty rings that usually hold his feeding dish. He had tried to go through it, but then decided to back up which resulted in one wing on top and the other on the bottom. He seemed quite calm, but I was in a panic. I had no idea how to get him out and I just knew I was going to get a bad bite trying. I held a towel below to cradle him while I unscrewed the ring from the outside of the cage. I set both on the floor and Pickles started to squirm so I covered him to calm him while I figured out what to do. When I lifted the towel to begin, I was greeted with "Well hello there!" He had freed himself somehow and had come to the conclusion that this was just a fun game. We have since removed all rings, in all cages, that aren't big enough for him to crawl through. This situation could have been much worse had Pickles panicked. He could have lost a wing.

24

Shortly after our incident, three guys wandered into the shop, complaining they hadn't been catching fish the last couple of days. I stood behind the counter, giving them suggestions for flies that might work for them and they just grumbled that none of them were working. I was still shaken by our little incident earlier, had a hard time concentrating and was in no mood for miserable fishermen but I took a deep breath and started to say "Why don't you try …" when suddenly Pickles piped up with "Woolly Bugger".

One guy looked at me, laughed and said, "We don't use Woolly Buggers, they're just searching patterns." I chuckled and said, "I didn't say you should."

"Yes you did" he argued, "You just said that."

"Nooooo" I said, "HE said it" and pointed behind me.

"Who?!" he asked, looking like he thought I'd lost my mind.

I turned around to show him but there was no bird in sight. Pickles was hiding in his little play box and I'm left looking like some batty fly shop lady.

I told them there's a bird in the box but they weren't buying it so I called Pickles. No answer.

The guys are looking for an escape route.

"Pickles!" No answer.

I walked over, peered in the box but Pickles is just laying on his belly, bobbing his head at me. I put my hand inside to bring him out but he gently took my finger in his beak and pushed it aside.

25

"Oh you little stinker" I said, "Tell me what's working Pickles."

"Woolly Bugger" says the wooden house.

"SEE?" I exclaimed.

"YOU said that!" they insisted.

Crap.

Time for drastic measures. "Daddy's home!" I hollered with excitement and out pops a head saying "Huh?"

"THERE! SEE?" I ask them.

"Is that a REAL bird?" one asks.

"Forget it" I said and went out on the floor to help them, thinking these guys are thick.

Most people got a kick out of Pickles and Pickles fit right in with the fly shop. He seldom disappointed anyone with his antics and he enjoyed the social interaction. I think it really helped him in becoming a well-balanced, albeit pushy, bird. Later on, he would start picking and choosing the days he wanted to come to work. I guess everybirdy needs a day off sometimes.

Chapter 3

The Yard and The Neighborhood

Months had gone by and it was like Pickles had been with us forever. Everything was going well. I had purchased a screened bird backpack and Pickles would go for walks with us or sometimes just shopping. He loved accompanying me to the grocery store and while in the produce isle, would pipe up "Wanna buy a bean." Green beans were his food of choice these days.

He was quick to chat it up with people and that was often embarrassing because Pickles was behind me so people in front thought I was talking to myself and making strange noises. For weeks, he had been making weird beeping noises but only while in the grocery store. I didn't know what it was until one day, while standing in line at the check out till; the sound was coming from both infront and behind me. He had picked up the sounds of the lottery terminal and the clerks found this highly entertaining.

Pickles would willingly get in his backpack or recently purchased travel cage. He was interested in seeing new places. This included our trips to lake cabins for our fishing trips. By now, we had 3 different cages other than his travel cage and backpack. We would set up a cage at the cabin, next to a window so that Pickles could watch the wildlife. He loved to watch all the birds and bugs and quickly picked up 4 different loon calls. He would announce to us "There's a bug!" if one flew by and this included hummingbirds. We would correct him but he was pretty sure that anything that small, had to be a bug.

Pickles is a good traveler and he loves new places and new scenery. This was a blessing since we spent so much time staying in cabins, tents or our RV and fishing different lakes. He was perfectly happy to be set up in a window where he could not only watch nature, but also watch us in our boats on the water. We never went far enough that we couldn't keep an eye on him, in case there were bird thieves in the area, and we could always hear him.

We're not bird watchers in the sense that we take our binoculars everywhere and hunt around for different species but we take great pleasure in watching the wild birds around us and everything else that nature provides. There's nothing better than waking deep in the outdoors. You lay there, still dozing, reluctant to rise and dreading the alarm clock. Slowly your eyes flutter open and reality sets in. You're not at home! You're at the lake!

A small campfire comforts you as you sip your coffee in your favorite torn and tattered Lumberman's jacket. Coffee taste so much better in the crisp, clean air just as the sun rises. You know with certainty there's a lake only feet from where you sit but it's hidden by the mist rising from the water. You know there's fish because you can hear the soft splashes as they sip the morning chironomids off the surface.

A sigh escapes your lips as the sun slowly makes it appearance, struggling to free itself from beyond the grassy hillside; glorious colors bathe the sky and blanket the ground around you, giving the grass a soft velvety appearance. Whisky Jacks, the friendliest birds in the forest, are gliding into your campsite to perch patiently in hopes of breakfast. Beef Jerky is the only food within reach and before you can rip it from its package an especially friendly Jack is poised on your knee awaiting a morsel. Unbelievable! You're so caught up in the moment that you don't care that you've just fed $20.00 worth of Jerky to your feathered friends.

28

What's that noise?! Huge buzzing mosquitos? Ahhh, hummingbirds! At least a dozen, tiny delicate bodies hovering and dive-bombing each other in competition for the sugary water you've hung in the nearby Lodgepole tree. The sun glances off their chests reflecting brilliant colors like cut crystal, colors you never knew existed. One bird dives out of nowhere, a direct hit on an unsuspecting hummer sitting and feeding contently on his perch. He falls to the ground as your heart sinks with him. Collecting his little body and cupping him in your palm, you realize he is merely stunned. He sits, all fluffed up in a little ball, staring into your face. You're certain that when he comes to his senses he will spear you with his needle-like beak, but he doesn't. A few minutes pass, a final glance and he's up, up and away.

Breakfast is a leisurely meal consisting of overcooked bacon and eggs accompanied by burnt campfire toast. Delicious! By the second cup of coffee the lake is making it's appearance from below the mist. Almost reluctantly you begin to unpack your gear and put your rods together. After much anguishing over the fly box, an interesting looking maroon sparkle leech is chosen to grace the end of your sinking line. A good pattern to start with, good for searching out fish.

On the way to the boat launch you stop at the spawning channel. You're feeling a little like a voyeur but the feeling quickly passes as you get caught up in the dance of the fish. One female, balanced on her side, violently thrashes the gravel bottom with her tail over and over, desperately working on the perfect bed to lay her eggs. A large, hook jawed male valiantly chases off would-be suitors and displays the wounds of previous battles. Time to go, a little privacy here please.

A quick check of the shoreline is proof that you could not have picked a better time for this fishing trip. Scuds in olives and browns as big as your thumbnail are swimming in clouds. Mayfly nymphs skitter to and fro, damsel nymphs swimming snake-like towards the weed beds and clinging to the weeds, clouds of them having already emerged are rising from the tall grass, caddis pupa on the move and a lone Gomphus dragonfly nymph waiting in ambush behind a submerged rock. No sign of emerging chironomids, just scattered shucks of all sizes on the surface - that's okay, the rest can't stay down forever.

Pushing off from the shoreline, the water is calm as glass as you head for the nearest drop-off dragging a leech pattern just off the bottom. What was that??? A hit! Already?! Raising the rod tip the line goes slack - probably bottom. Strip in the line, check the fly, back in the water and off you go again. Wham! Now THAT'S a hit! Rod tip up - too late. Strip the line in, check the fly; back in the water and off you.........there it is again! Raise the rod tip, line is taut this time as a nice chrome 22 incher explodes out of the water - he lands with a less than elegant splash, dives, takes a run for it, peeling off line so fast you're afraid he'll smoke the old reel. Suddenly nothing. Is he gone? No! He's heading straight toward you in leaps and bounds along the surface! NOBODY can strip THAT fast! He dives, only to reappear seconds later 4 feet from your nose. Seemingly suspended mid-air, in slow motion you watch him spit the hook and roll his eyes at you as he sinks into the depths leaving you looking like a drowned rat. As you regain you composure you start to laugh, well THAT was fun!

The rest of the cruise is uneventful and upon arriving at the chosen drop-off time is spent casting into the shallows with absolutely no action. Your mind drifts as all the worries and cares of everyday life flow from your body in pleasant little waves. The sky is partially clouded, weather is warm and you can't ever remember feeling so content.

Thoughts are scattered as 2 mating loons catch your attention about 100 feet away. They bob and rise, twist and turn, dive and re emerge, flap their wings and dance across the water in perfect unison, looking amazingly like a mirror image. The show ends as they head across the lake, half flying, half running across the water and out of sight.

30

Reflecting on nature, you've unknowingly drifted into the shallows and find yourself gazing into the clear water. Looky, looky! Fish! Lots of them! Cruising in less than 5 feet of water. Sticklike creatures are poking up everywhere along the surface - chronies! A quick inspection reveals an assorted mixture of colors and sizes, it's a free-for-all! How to choose?! Starting with a size 16 redbutt, changing to a size 14 pheasant tail then moving on to a size 12 chromie produces nothing but the odd tap. Oh hell, just leave it out there and wait.

While you're waiting you notice the most perfect piece of land right in front of you. Before long, you've built a modest little cabin nestled in the trees - just enough trees to partially seclude you from prying, envious eyes but not enough to block the sun. The quaint little porch is graced with the most rickety, but comfortable, old rocking chairs. A beaten path leads to the T-shaped floating dock with lots of room for a back cast. Maybe one day the dream will become reality.

What an interesting statue. Right there where the dock should be. Holy cow, it's a heron. Watching...watching...why, it hasn't moved a muscle for at least 10 minutes, I wonder how long...whoops, missed a hit, strip the line in fast so I can get back to watching the heron...wham! Hard hit! Hurry! Hurry haaard! A couple of good runs, couple of dives, still haven't seen him but he's ready to come in. Ahhhh, beauuuuty! Slide the barbless hook out nice and easy, release him gently into the water and off he goes - 18 inches maybe, and fat. Damn, you look up just in time to see a small fish disappearing down the throat of the heron.

Swoooosh, SPLASH! What the hell was THAT?! You turn and look just as an osprey is beating its wing along the water surface and rising, rising into the sky with a fish bigger than the one you just released. He banks hard to the left and you notice why. A bald headed eagle has taken up the chase. The osprey ducks and dodges, finally makes it into the cover of the forest. The eagle gives up, heads high into the sky and hovers. He starts to drop, nope, changes his mind, back into position. A minute later - nose down, he dives like a missile, faster and faster then

31

just feet from the water he jams on the brakes, pulls out, glides along the surface and starts his ascent to search once again.

An hour goes by, then another. No more action. Doesn't matter. The scenery is spectacular and wildlife abounds. Ducks with adorable little ducklings learning to dive and popping back up out of the water like little rubber balls. Bossy geese and their goslings. A muskrat momentarily entangled in your floating line. No bear, deer or moose but then you already saw a bear and her cub and a white tailed deer on the drive in. Only one fish landed but it wasn't even the highlight. It was just one great part of this most memorable day.

On the way in, dragging that same leech again, a nice little 14 incher is brought to the boat - perfect for the fry pan! Back to camp and a fresh air nap. Salivating as the fresh trout sizzles in the fire, wafting it's delicate scent your way now and then. Paprika, garlic, onion-fried potatoes to accompany the fish and an ice-cold beer.

The sky erupts into brilliant colors of blood reds and fiery oranges as the sun retires for the evening. Red sky at night, fishermen's delight - a delightful sign of the next day to come. The owl in the tree overhead hoots softly as you drift off in your lawn chair thinking - life just doesn't get any better than this.

Sorry, I get a little carried away when I start thinking of nature.

There are 2 people I have to credit for my love of birds. First - my mom. As a kid, I was always interested in birds, along with any sort of animal and creature. When I was young, she taught me to respect animals and wildlife and my parents always allowed us to have pets. My entire life, I kept animals of some sort but at some point I kind of lost touch with nature and the wild and I blame my Grandmother for that. She was a teacher – a very serious and strict one. She lived in Saskatchewan so mom would have all us kids write to her but she always sent my letter back, corrected. She would underline all my spelling and grammar mistakes and put a grade at the top of the page – anything from a 'D' to and 'A'. An 'A' grade was accompanied by a star sticker. I found out in later years that she did the same to my mom, even as an adult. As a young teenager, I stopped writing to her because it made me so angry.

When she came to visit, or if we went to visit her, a lot of our time was spent taking walks. Walks were fine by me but she would insist on stopping to look at every plant, tree, animal or bird and then lecture us with information about it. When we returned home, I was basically given a test on what we had learned that day. She would have collected specimens such as leaves, flowers or branches then produce the items and have us identify them. Soon, I refused to go with walks with her. It was just too much like homework and I got enough of that at school, which I hated.

One year, we went to visit for a couple of weeks at Christmas time and I thought that was wonderful because I was excused from my school for a whole week. Once there, I was informed that I would be attending her class and I thought it might be cool, something different and I'd be the teacher's pet since she was my Grandma. Not to be. I was picked on mercilessly. I was asked to answer every question directed to the class, even if others had their hands up. I was chided for not answering correctly and was even shamed by being ordered to stand in a corner. My excuse that I hadn't learned these things in my class at school wasn't even considered.

Many years later, Neil and I took my mom to camp in an RV next to a lake for a couple of weeks. Mom brought her bird identification book and insisted on including me in her page flipping identifications any time a bird was spotted. I was there to relax and just enjoy my surroundings and suddenly, there I was, doing homework again. I tried to humor her but I was seething inside.

33

The next time Neil and I went camping, alone, we started noticing birds and wondering what they were. Suddenly I was wishing I had paid attention with mom and started to feel bad about my behavior. I also started regretting that I hadn't listened to my Grandma because now I wanted to know everything about anything to do with nature. Mom hadn't forced the bird thing on me; she had just wanted someone to enjoy it with. That one trip with her though, brought nature crashing back to me.

A few years later, it was Pickles who had credit due. How can you live with a bird and not start appreciating any other kind of bird? You see that they have character and personality and you start to wonder how that applies to wild birds. You start looking at all birds in a different light and appreciating both their similarities and their differences. They stop being just these little creatures flying about.

Pickles is happy watching nature and our yard is almost as good as the wild. He likes spending time with us outside and there's always something to observe. The first couple of years, we put him in a cage outside but after awhile it cramped his style so an aviary was built. We have a yard that is just slightly larger than average and we've planted over 150 trees and shrubs for wild bird habitat. Over the years, Pickles had developed an incredible repertoire of birdcalls but his favorite bird, and his favorite bird sound is the crow. He gets very excited when they're around and caws insistently at them. The crows basically ignore him but the chickadees like to visit him now and then.

Pickles' sole purpose in life is to abuse people and embarrass me. Pickles outside, is a disaster waiting to happen. One day, Pickles and I are hanging out in the aviary on a warm spring day. Pickles perches above, preening and content in the warm morning sunshine. Our yard is lovely in its semi-wild state and flocks of Evening Grosbeaks are frolicking. Trees and shrubs dot the long, semi-circle perimeter of the yard. People walking by briefly appear and disappear between the foliage due to the gaps of a mere foot or two between the outer border of trees.

34

An old man strolls by, lost in thought, appearing here and there between the perimeter trees. As he appears between the first gap in the shrubbery, Pickles spots him and greets him with "Hellooooooo". The man's startled face glances up just as it's disappearing behind the next bush. "Hello" says the bush. A moment later the man appears on the other side.

The old man stops, smiling and ready to engage in neighborly conversation but there's nobody to be seen in the yard. Looking a little embarrassed, he turns to continue his walk. Now, all this happens in an instant so before I can respond, and as he is disappearing behind the next bush, Pickles inquires "Aren't cha hungry?"

"What?" asks the bush. When the man comes out from behind, he doesn't stop this time. He only slows down while his eyes dart around, desperately looking for the source of the voice. Again, just as he's walking behind the next bush, Pickles calls out "Doncha want sum breakfast?"

This time, as the man comes out from behind a bush, I wave and say "Over here!" But he's picked up his pace. Although he's looking in the yard, he doesn't have time to spot me before the next bush, or the one after … or after that … because now he's practically running. I'm only catching quick glimpses of a scared little old man. He's gone. High tailed it right on out of there with Pickles screaming after him …"Want some pom pom breakfast?" (pomegranate) "Eat your breakfast!"

I was standing in the middle of the yard by then and before I can recover from my dismay and embarrassment, a car goes by. Inside are two young men, cruising slowly, arms out the windows, moving to the music. Pickles lets out a loud wolf whistle. I'm praying they don't hear it over the loud music, but I never seem to have that kind of luck where Pickles is concerned. And sure enough, I hear the car stop and back up. They find a gap in the trees, where they can see me. I'm horrified.

"Sorry. That was my parrot", I explain as I point toward the aviary. "Oh" the driver says, "Cool." But I don't think they believed me, and you could see the disappointment in their faces that I wasn't some hot young chick. Then, just as they start to drive away, Pickles hollers "Score!" Oh man ... I'm dying here. However, I was thankful that they were out of earshot when Pickles did his loud Bull Frog. It sounds more like flatulence. Thank God for small favors.

"My God Pickles!" I exclaim, "You are SO embarrassing, I could wring your little neck!"

"Take your pills." He said.

The neighbors get a real kick out of him though and Jeff, from across the street, likes to whistle back and forth with him. Pickles likes it when Jeff copies everything he does and Pickles tries to trip him up. Sometimes it works and we hear Jeff say "Well, you got me there. I can't do that." Jeff's a good whistler so Pickles also likes to try and copy him. That's good because I don't whistle all that well, Neil can't whistle at all so Pickles has to rely on TV and making up his own tunes, which he is very good at.

Our neighbor Dave, right next door, sometimes gets the brunt of Pickles' cruelness. Dave was painting his back porch one day and Pickles' play stand is next to the window, overlooking Dave's back yard, so Pickles made the sound of a phone ringing through the open (but screened) window. Dave dropped everything and ran in the house to answer his phone. A minute later, he returned and Pickles rang the phone again. Dave obliged Pickles by running back in the house. Several rings later, Dave finally noticed Pickles and realized he'd been duped.

Pickles doesn't fool us too often anymore because we realized he needs to answer his own phone. He has the spacing between rings perfect but after 2 or 3 rings, he can't help but go "Beep. Hello?" So, we wait. He also physically pretends to pick up the receiver. He raises his little talon up to his ear as he says "Hello?" and has his own little conversation. "Uhuh. Okay. Uhuh. Okay then, bye-bye." Then he lowers his talon, effectively hanging up the receiver.

Dave had a collie over for a play date with his golden retriever and Pickles got a kick out of watching them play. As the dogs were play fighting, Pickles would bark and all play would stop while the dogs looked around for the intruder. Unable to find the culprit, they continued with their play. Pickles continued this game until I thought the poor dogs would go mad.

We spend a lot of time in our yard and wanted to add a water feature to attract more birds so we decided to build a pond. Our trout permit finally arrived from the Ministry of Environment so we bought fish and released them into their new home. We took Pickles out to the aviary for his supper and settled next to the pond in lawn chairs to observe our trout.

Everything was going just fine – Pickles went on and on about his supper. "Supper in the aviary. Mmmmmmm. What a good supper. Mmmmmmm."

Two young girls, about 16 years old, walked down the side of the road about 25 feet from Pickles. Naturally, Pickles feels required to act neighborly. His hellos draw no response and he takes rejection personal so he resorts to loud whistling. The girls glance around but keeping walking. As I mentioned earlier, the aviary is sort of hidden and it's difficult to see an African Gray in an 8X8 structure of branches through our yard foliage.

Whistling obviously wasn't good enough so he hollers out "Gimme kiss!" which makes the girls giggle uncomfortably since all they could see was Neil and I sitting pond side. They continued on their way and I thought nothing of it until Neil said that they might have thought it was he talking to them since Pickles speaks in Neil's voice most times. I began to cringe out of embarrassment but tried to put it out of my mind and watch the fish.

A few minutes later, the girls came back. I was just heading into the house but stopped, figuring I'd set this right so I called out "Did you hear him say he wanted a kiss?" pointing at the corner of the aviary where Pickles sat, quiet for once.

One of the girls glanced over at me with a mixed look of disgust, shock, and horror. I was appalled to be on the receiving end of such a look.

"It was the parrot asking for a kiss!" I called out again but the girls had their heads together, talking and hurrying away. They didn't hear me.

"Way to go" Neil said. "You told them it was HIM and pointed in the general direction of both of us. They think you were talking about *me*!"

I replayed it in my mind and yup, that's exactly the way it would have looked. Now they think I'm some weird old lady that wants them to kiss some lecherous old man. Sometimes I think about buying Pickles a muzzle.

We spend as much time as possible, sitting around the pond. It's about 20 feet long, 16 feet wide with waterfall and rocky shoal gradually sloping to its 5-foot depth. The waterfall, fed through the pump in the deepest end, helps provide aeration and filtration.

You can't help but fixate on the waterfall, the water gracefully cascading down the rocks and navigating the short creek until tapering elegantly into the shallows, where little trout sit in anticipation of drifting food. The pleasing tone of a babbling brook is utterly mesmerizing and transcending.

Rocks of all sizes are handpicked for their unique color or shape and placed along the perimeter of the pond. Thyme, yarrow and wildflowers creep through the rocks and naturally envelope the pond while the trees reflect their colorful foliage on the glassy surface below. Unsuspecting insects land on the water and fish rise for the offering. As the fish are dining, the waterfall and shoal are alive with birds of all sizes taking their evening bath. And all the while, the songbirds in the trees are in perfect harmony with the silvery song of the brook. Now and then, Pickles notices a fish take an insect off the surface and will alert us with "Fishy eat a bug!"

Our yard is a jungle with trees, shrubs, vegetable garden and even a couple of piles of discarded tree prunings. We continue piling on to them as this makes great bird habitat, providing shelter, nesting and foraging. There are little benches or seats tucked into sheltered areas and a trail system is slowly developing as foliage grows and we add more trees or shrubs.

We stopped using poisons in our yard about 12 years ago. The birds thank us, and so do the dandelions. To be perfectly honest, I like dandelions and I think they got a bad rep as a weed. We've found that most weeds have beneficial properties, from medicinal to edible so we don't sweat it – we use what we grow, or it's put in the trusty composter.

I don't think our neighbors are pleased with us. We let our grass grow, we have dandelions, I think we play our music too loud, they're leery of the bat boxes and they assume our pond breeds mosquitoes. We've tried to tell them, if you let your grass grow, you don't have to water so much and it will eventually choke out the dandelions. Bats are good. Contrary to popular belief, they don't attack hair and they eat the mosquitoes. The fish are the best thing to happen to the neighborhood because the water attracts the little blood suckers, providing meals for the fish.

39

The mosquitoes can't breed in the pond because it's too deep and too fast. As for the loud music, well, we keep working on that.

We spent a lot of time camping and fishing most of our lives but after spending so much time watching our fish, it's difficult for us now. In the early days of fishing, we killed them for food. I'm not comfortable killing anything but it's either that, or buy it in a can. A fish is going to die, one way or another when I'm in the mood to eat fish. In later years, we became catch & release fishermen as conservation started to demand. I was never quite comfortable with that, it just didn't seem right to go and stress a fish out for our own pleasure. Now, after getting to know our fish, we realize that they possess little personalities and that they're not just some dumb creatures beneath the sea. We will continue to fish, but rarely, and we seek other species of fish for table fare.

We rarely feel the need to go camping and wildlife watching because we have just as much nature in our own back yard. Sometimes we 'pretend fish'. We both pick a fly that's landed on the water and see whose is eaten first. It's just as fun as real fishing; the only difference is that the fly is not attached to the end of a line.

The yard and pond is a constant source of entertainment and it illustrates the importance of every single creature, and the fact that they all have personalities, intelligence and adventurous lives. There was a blue dragonfly that came to visit the pond every day for a few weeks, hovering or flitting around the pond, catching midges that were hatching from the water. One day, a green dragonfly appeared and you could literally see the excitement from both of them upon discovering each other. The entered into a lovely, graceful aerial dance, then a game of tag and at one point one of them managed to hide behind the reeds. I watched him hover in one spot, only turning slightly now and then to watch the other through the reed blades. After a minute or so, the other one thought to come around the plant and the moment she discovered him, they both danced in the air with glee. Imagine, bugs playing hide-and-go-seek!

Fish themselves are reduced to a commodity and we just see them as a massive lump in a seine net or food in a can but each fish had an adventurous life before that. They also have friends. The other day, I watched one of our trout holding next to a plant in the shallows while he let 3 different fish into the area, to swim, hunt and even nudge him but the minute one particular fish attempted to swim by; he dashed after him and refused to let him in the area. They obviously make distinctions between friends and foes.

The yard is our sanctuary and it's a wonderful distraction for Pickles. It is peaceful, yet alive. Because we spend all our time out there, all visitors are dragged out with us. So, when my mom came to visit one spring, we all spent a lot of time in the yard.

Her grandchildren call my mother, who by now is Pickles' biggest fan, "Nana" but Pickles prefers to call her "Nana Banana". She has a hard time concentrating on anything else but Pickles while she's here and especially loves it when Pickles is chatting to invisible characters in his Fun Factory. This is a plastic globe that hangs from the ceiling with holes in the side for climbing in and out. She likes to relax and read while here but I'm sure she only succeeds in reading the same page over and over because mostly I see her looking over the top of her book at Pickles.

Pickles likes my mom but back then they didn't get too close ever since she showed up one time in her coat of many colors – mostly reds. It was "scary" as Pickles would tell you, and for while he was a little leery of getting too close to Mom in case that coat may still be hidden upon her person. Mom sometimes animates with her arms and hands while telling a story, so that too can be "scary" when you're half asleep and sitting on the knee of the animator. Regardless, he's always happy to see her and doesn't hesitate to chat it up with her. She even started to call before her visits, to discuss her wardrobe … "Does Pickles like orange? Can I wear my flowered pajamas? What about hats?" Etc.

41

Mom wrote a cute poem in Pickles' Christmas card one year, entitled The Pickles Bird's Christmas Present …

What a nice song" you could hear people say,
From the first thing Christmas morning, til the end of the day.

And the Pickles Bird sat on the bells and the horns
And he bobblebird danced all Christmas morn.

"See the present! Oh my! Must we wait to begin it?"
Cause he knew it was his – whatever was in it.

So the Pickles Bird pulled and the Pickles Bird tugged
Til he tipped over backwards and fell on the rug.

He pulled and he pushed and he blonked and he bleaked.
He picked at the billball and fell on his beak.

He scuffled and scorted. He screed and he skried
And suddenly quick as a Whifflepuff's cry,
Out fell the prize. My, My, and Oh My!

And what was this wonderful, wonderful thing?
A Sondercubs triss or a Whipnubbers bling?

A Whirlykaboodle brings anyone joy.
No! A Special Kermuffly Pickles Bird Toy.

Move over Dr. Seuss.

It's a good thing my mother is not a prude. Right off the bat, we were throwing little whiffle balls to Pickles on the back of the couch and as he snagged one in the air with his talon, it caused him to flip over on his back, wedging him against the wall. "Oh shit!" he exclaimed as he struggled to right himself. That was the very first time he had uttered these words and thankfully, he seldom repeats it.

Pickles loves to fool my mom by ringing the phone and she falls for it most times. If she doesn't, he calls out "Answer the damn bird!"

We celebrated my mom's birthday while she was here and even though the word 'party' was never mentioned, Pickles somehow senses the days we plan to have a couple of drinks and play music. Perhaps it's because he sees us making ice. He joins in with the sound of tinkling ice cubes, the snap of the pop can being opened and the fizzling of the soda – which he calls "juice". Then Pickles suggests the perfect place for the party ...

"Anybody in the aviary? Wanna party? Wanna party in the aviary? Want music in the aviary? Let's go party in the aviary! Let's go, let's go, let's go, let's go!"

The three of us agree, so we made Pina Coladas, put on Pickles favorite fiddle music and packed him out to the yard while he showed his appreciation with "Woo Hoo! What a good song! Sing a song with your beak!"

Neil grabbed the hose to water the herbs and inadvertently sprayed Pickles. This was NOT a part of the deal and he ran along his perches, flapping his wings angrily, hollering "Uh oh. Uh oh. Uh oh. Stop it! Just stop it! Stop it brat!" Neil stopped and apologized but Pickles' good mood was ruined ... until a neighbor who'd never met Pickles spotted us and came over to chat with him. A new victim caused Pickles to snap out of his snit and when the fellow said, "Well now, what do we have in here?" Pickles answered ...

43

"Freshwater rat baby!"

During this period, Pickles' favorite word was 'rat' and he had become quite fond of adding 'ary' to his words.

"Hello rat baby! Want some rat beans? Want some rat poop? Poop on the rats. Go poop. Poop in the rat aviary for a snack. Wanna go in the aviary? Want some snackery in the aviary? Wanna bananary in the aviary? There's a buggery in the aviary! Hafta poopery in the aviary? Huh?"

"rrrrrrrats"

The neighbor looked at us, looked at Pickles and back at us.

"I don't know this bird." I said. "He wandered in the yard one day, we fed him and now he won't go away."

Chapter 4

Not Always Fun & Games

Birds poop, a lot. No getting around it. If you own a bird, it's something you learn to put up with. In the wild, they poop to get rid of the extra baggage for fast take-off, flight and safety. Over time, Pickles got pretty good about holding it and not just releasing his bombs all helter skelter but there were many episodes early on. Poop decorated floors, furniture and clothing. I don't know how many times I've been out in public only to return home and discover a nice gooey blob on my arm, shoulder or chest that I hadn't noticed before I left the house. Nobody ever says anything. They can't help but see it but you're not given the chance to explain – no, I didn't just hork all over myself.

Pickles turned out to be a very finicky eater so we were always looking for new and innovative ways to get him to eat the things that were good for him. Like most parrots, he showed his displeasure by throwing food. We didn't always have the time to clean up after him so his cage, the walls and the floor were sometimes mottled with dried up scraps of food. He thought nothing of flinging undesired food in our faces and stomping around on the top of his cage, throwing a temper tantrum.

I learned to make birdy breads. They are sort of like carrot cake and I add different items of fruits and vegetables to each one so that he gets the proper vitamins and nutrients he requires. It's very time consuming between baking them and cutting them up in rows of little squares, wrapping with saran wrap, labeling

45

then freezing. But Pickles loves them and he gets a square each night for supper. Over time, he got use to the taste of most fruits and veggies and will sometimes eat them fresh now, but not much. His favorites are bananas, grapes, pomegranate, carrots, potatoes and pepper seeds. Breakfast is fresh peas or corn and during the day he gets pellets, seeds and nuts. He's a healthy, active bird so I guess we're doing something right.

Fortunately, we live in an arid area of the BC Interior and have no problem with mold or mildew. We can leave fruits or vegetables in Pickles' bowl for longer periods of time than someone living in a humid climate – everything just sort of dries up, like sun drying a tomato. We don't have to worry about mold on his cage however, things can dry to a dust and cause respiratory problems.

On the other hand, humidity would be good for Pickles because he hates to bathe and he's a dirty, dirty little birdie. He freaks out if we use a spray bottle and mostly he just gets his feet and beak wet on the odd occasion that he takes a bath in a bowl. The only humidity he gets, is from taking showers with Neil. He likes to perch on the shower rod and watch but doesn't like to be splashed. Sometimes we'll bend over the kitchen sink and Pickles will run up and down our arms to get a little wet under the tap.

At some point, it became difficult to keep Pickles aloft. He was insisting on climbing down his cage to explore, or to be with us. Often, he was almost stepped on when he suddenly appeared at our feet while we were off doing something. It was becoming dangerous in the shop with customers walking around and it seemed there was no way to make him stay put.

I won't go into many details or the complications of this and other behavioral problems but what it boiled down to was finding the PBAS (Parrot Behavior Analysis Solutions) Group where they pair you with someone to help and interact with you on a forum or through email. They teach Positive Reinforcement which has become a way of life for us with Pickles. Pickles is never punished, parrots don't understand punishment, it just causes dislike, distrust or fear. He is rewarded for good behavior and bad behavior is ignored. All it takes is a little creative thinking to make a parrot feel that he is in control, and reinforcers such as food or toys are used as encouragement.

PBAS taught us the importance of enrichment and foraging so Neil got busy making play stands for Pickles. He started by building a wooden base with 4-inch lip all the way around, which gave Pickles something to sit on, and attached legs like you find on a computer chair in the center so that Pickles couldn't reach and climb down. To the base, he attached a few thick branches with thinner branches shooting off the main branch, providing him a variety of perches and climbing material. From these, we hung various toys. Neil built several stands so that Pickles would have an area in each room to hang out on while we did dishes or ate dinner etc. Each one was different and he was happy to be moved from room to room to be with us. The main play stand was placed next to Pickles' cage in the livingroom so that he had access to it whenever he wanted.

Our lovely home became one big birdcage, still void of paintings or knick knacks that we felt needed protection from Pickles. We may as well have replaced the couches with stick furniture and the carpets with cement flooring and put in a drain so that we could hose the house down to clean all the spattered poop and food as needed.

It took a couple of weeks of working with PBAS but various plans were implemented, success was achieved and it has stuck with him for the most part. There is still the very, very odd time that Pickles, if left alone too long, will climb down and go searching for us. Sometimes he might be startled into flying down but he has become uncomfortable on the floor so he will quickly scramble back up his cage.

47

Pickles has always been afforded a lot of freedom, meaning a lot of time out of his cage. About the only time he was required to be caged was at bedtime or if we had to go out. He started refusing to go in the cage when we needed to go out and as I said earlier, we don't like to force him into anything. To make matters worse, he was now deciding which days he wanted to go to work with us. Some days, he preferred to stay home and refused to get in his travel cage to go with us. The first couple of times this happened, he wouldn't go in his living room cage so we had to trick him by placing his favorite foods inside and locking the cage door after he climbed in. He caught on fast and stopped going in after the food.

I was desperate one day. Neil was out of town and I had to open the shop. Pickles didn't want to go to work, and didn't want to go in his cage. After trying unsuccessfully to bribe him, I finally had to leave. I came home part way through the day to check on him, it's only a 2-minute drive, and everything seemed fine but he still wouldn't get in his cage. When I got home that night, he was whistling happily on his cage top and there were no signs of destruction or tell tale signs of poop on floors or furniture. Since Pickles, by this time, was not all that destructive and preferred staying aloft, we figured we'd let him have his way until we came up with a better plan.

Still though, there were days he was good about going in the cage and I had no problem locking him in so one day I had some shopping to do and was gone for about 45 minutes. Upon my return, I thought it curious that I wasn't greeted with Pickles' usual "Mama's home! Hello baby!" so I walked into the living room to investigate.

My heart sank to the pit of my stomach as I realized my very, very, VERY worst fear had become a reality. I stood, dumbfounded, gaping at an empty cage. Somebody broke in the house and stole him.

48

Then I noticed the cage door. hmmm. What kinda self-respecting thief would steal a parrot and take the time to lock the cage door in the open position? Damn, I'd gone out and forgot to put Pickles in his cage. My relief quickly turned to worry though because he wasn't anywhere in sight.

I began my search, looking for signs of a poop trail. I'm calling for him and his silence conjures up images of an electrified bird lying in a smoking heap behind the couch (having chewed through an electric cord). My grasping mind tells me "it's okay, you know how he clams up in impish delight while enjoying an impromptu game of hide-and-seek" but I'm uneasy non-the-less.

As I'm on my hands and knees, peering under a couch, I hear a VERY distinctive nose laugh. You know the sound - when someone is laughing through their nose with their mouth closed. I look up from my crouched position, into the kitchen about 6 feet away and there, smack dab in the middle of the dictionary stand, roosts a smartass little Grey.

"Pickles!" I exclaim.

"What's up?" he queries with a twinkle in his eye.

"I've been looking all over for you!" I reply.

"Huh?" he asks.

"You heard me." I said, which triggers more nose laughing and some gleeful head bobbing.

As I walked toward him he commanded, "Step up" as his little footsie was waving in the air in anticipation of my hand and a free ride home - or so I thought.

49

The moment he stepped up on my hand, he flung himself upside down exclaiming "Upside down bird!" I told him to get back up as I righted him with my other hand. After momentarily obliging, he promptly fell over once again. He thought this a delightful little game and continued to fall over like some stinkin' drunk.

So there I am, walking around with an upside down bird on my hand, telling him to get back up and he's piping "get back up!" right back at me. I carry this lippy, drunken bird to the cage and try to set him down gently on his back but he just lies there clinging to my finger. I try to pry his talons off but they just dig in deeper.

I give up, sit on the couch and place him on his back in my lap, between my legs. He lies there, trying to outlast me. Eventually he says "ticko, ticko, ticko" so I tickle his belly. He gets so excited that he releases his hold but is now stuck on his back like a turtle, waving his feet frantically in the air. I don't help the little stinker. Instead, I sit there and nose laugh.

All this time I had thought Pickles was getting his vocabulary from me. As it turned out, he'd been reading the dictionary behind my back.

I think the most serious issue was about 2 years after we got him, when Pickles started to bite Neil. He was biting hard and drawing blood any time Neil tried to get him to step up. There were 2 reasons we believe were the cause. I had come out from behind the counter at the shop one day to help someone choose some flies and another customer ducked behind the counter and got Pickles to step up. He moved fast for a large, imposing looking man and I didn't have time to react. By the time I got to him, Pickles was running up his arm and the man was grabbing his beak and teasingly shaking Pickles head. Pickles didn't like this and he bit, but this guy just thought it was funny and kept doing it. I got Pickles off the guy's arm as soon as I got there but the harm had been done.

From that moment, Pickles would talk to men but he didn't like being too close and would not step up for them, and this included Neil. Neil became quite fearful of Pickles and of course, Pickles picked up on this. He would offer Neil his neck for scratches but when Neil went to oblige, Pickles would whip his head around and bite – hard.

Around the same time, Neil had taken a 6-month job out of town, which meant he was only home for the odd weekend. During this time, Pickles bonded tight with me and Neil had become almost a stranger to him. It was frustrating for me when Neil came home to visit because, since he couldn't get close to Pickles there was little interaction between the two of them. Pickles had grown use to our routine of going for walks around the house or playing on the couch. He can be quite the card while playing and I would try to get Neil to watch but Neil was beginning to resent the time I spent with Pickles when he and I had so little time together these days. I was afraid their relationship was doomed for life, which wasn't fair for all involved.

I hatched a plan. Once he finished the out-of-town job, I made Neil Pickles' primary caregiver. Neil did all the feeding and all the cage cleaning. Pickles' favourite treats are pine nuts so Neil would drop them into Pickles' bowl or next to him throughout the day. Neil didn't get too close the first few days but made a point of standing next to Pickles just to chat. I taught Neil how to read Pickles body language so he could anticipate a bite and before long he was able to pick his moments and get Pickles to step up. All interaction with Pickles was to be fun, nothing negative and I handled any unpleasant situations that arose. Pickles soon learned that all interaction with Neil was fun and games and they bonded quickly. A few months later, Neil wrote an article for Good Bird Magazine entitled The Myth of One Person Birds. He wrote how to change it and how it's selfish not to. If something happens to a parrot's primary caregiver what becomes of that parrot? What kind of life will he have if he's incapable of bonding to anybody else?

51

A short time down the road, Neil had to go out of town again for 2 months and this time Pickles was miserable. If Pickles is miserable, I'm miserable. Not just because I feel sorry for him but also because the little snot is convinced it's entirely my fault so he rags on me all day. If parrots had their own swear words, his spiteful squawks would surely be unspeakable and when he does use his words, it's an insistent "Dadddeeeeeeeee. Daddy be right back!! Dadddeeeeeee. Daddy's home??? Dadddeeeeeee .....". I'd rather pluck nose hairs than listen to that.

Two nights after Neil's departure, Pickles is especially cranky. After an intense bout of the above behavior and mad at me for ignoring him, he stomped around the top of his cage attacking every single toy that had the nerve to cross his path then promptly ran down the outside cage bars and plopped his head into the outside pellet bowl. There he hung, clinging to the bars upside down with his head hidden like an ostrich in the dirt. He remained like that for quite some time completely motionless. I watched. He hung.

After awhile I finally asked if he was okay. An echoed grumbling was my only reply. A couple of minutes later, I asked again but his only response was a very quiet, mournful "Daddeeee" punctuated with a sigh.

"You gonna hang upside down with your head in a bowl for 2 months Pickles?" I asked.

"Stuck" he said.

"You're not stuck, your just sulking" I accused.

"STUCK" he insisted.

"Liar" I said.

A solitary eye rose barely above the brim just long enough to glare at me, then back to the bowl.

Fine, let's see how long he can pout upside down. I wait.

We both sit in silence. Blessed silence. Something I hadn't experienced for a couple of days.

Pickles couldn't stand it after awhile and couldn't resist raising his head in slow motion until one eyeball appeared just long enough to confirm he still had my attention. Then back in the bowl.

He soon tired of this position so, with his head still inside, one foot reached for the side of the bowl, but he slipped. With a flap and a squawk, he landed in the bowl with nothing but his little twinker sticking out.

A short struggle ensued and, without ever retracting his head, he managed a foothold on the edge of the bowl. There he perched, headless. And embarrassed. He blames the pellets and punishes them all by smashing them with his beak and sending them flying, head still in bowl.

He settles down but now it's a matter of pride. He's tired of his head in a bowl but how do you remove a head without losing face? He opts for a clever change of subject. Switching to his sweet voice, he politely asks, "Wanna sing a song?"

I'm tempted to make him sweat it out a little longer but I cave and sing him his favorite song. Up pops the weasel with a "Woo Hoo! Whatta good song!!" Pickles chimes in and we pretend he didn't just spend the last few minutes making a fool of himself.

He settled down after that but a couple of weeks later, I was sitting on the couch with Pickles on the back of the couch next to me. I noticed him looking with interest outside so I turned and saw the neighbour's headlights as he was turning into his driveway. I

commented, "Davie's home" and Pickles went ballistic! He started flapping, crouching, wing splaying and running back and forth the length of the window. In his excitement, he somehow became airborne and landed on the base of his play stand. From there, he scampered up the branches, fast as a monkey hollering "Daddy's home! Daddy's home! Woo hoo! Hello baby! Hello bayyyybeeee!"

Oh man, I felt sooo bad. He thought I said Daddy and even though he knows the difference in driveways I guess he got confused.

It took me awhile to calm him but after awhile he sat there, all fluffed up, mournfully informing me "Daddy go bye-bye. Be gone long."

Eventually Neil finished the job and returned home. The next day, he went to work at the shop, giving me the day off. Pickles wasn't happy.

"Daddy go bye-bye." he said glumly, "Be right back" he added.

I informed him "No, Daddy be gone long time."

Pickles whined, "Gone long time??"

"Yes" I answered.

Pickles firmly announced "He SAID he'd be right back!"

"He did not." I argued.

54

"He said he'd sing a song!" Pickles said.

"Stop lying Pickles, Daddy went to work." I insisted.

"What a load of beans" he spat.

I mentioned Pickles' little screech in the first chapter. Over time, that little screech may as well have been a drill through the head. I think I might have preferred it. He did it whenever he wasn't happy and usually, if Pickles wasn't happy, it was because he wasn't getting enough attention. At first, when he did this, we would tend to him and fix whatever was wrong. Bad mistake. Pickles learned that screeches were rewarded with attention so he used it incessantly. The more he used it, the more we tried to please him. We don't yell at Pickles, well that's not exactly true. We've yelled pretty loud, and let out some pretty good swear words but that's only while being on the bad end of a beak. But when he'd start in, we'd start in with the firm reprimands. Well! Pickles thought this grand! Any attention, ANY, was better than NONE!

But when you really take the time to think about these things, it's not hard to outwit a bird while allowing him to think he has the upper hand. It was hard, but from now on, the moment Pickles screeched, we would stand up and walk out of the room. He didn't like that. Not one bit. So, he'd scream bloody murder for our return. We would wait for the first moment of silence and then immediately return to the room and sit down. We never looked at him or talked to him on the way in or the way out. At first, he would start the screeching within the first minute or 2 so up we got and left the room again. It's hard to do this and hard to be consistent because it only takes giving in once for him to get his reward and revert back to his poor behaviour. That means starting all over. It's never convenient when you're absorbed in a TV show or you're eating dinner but it had to be done. He's a quick study once you come up with a plan. He soon learned that he didn't just have to be quiet, that a nice chirp or word could initiate our return.

So, that worked while we were in the room but what about when we were off doing something and Pickles was bored? He could stay quiet for only so long before he'd revert to screeching for us to give him some attention so we developed a little whistle. Neil couldn't join in on this plan because he can't whistle but I started waiting until he was quiet for a moment, then I'd whistle. Within an hour, he had the whistle down pat and we whistled to each other from separate rooms. Later, it became him asking "Anybody home?" and we would answer back "Everybody's home!" which resulted in a "Woo hoo!" and he'd either keep chatting with us or go back to whatever he was doing until the next time he wanted contact.

When we were busy, we would often make a point to stop and visit Pickles briefly to hand him a snack or toy. This would not only keep him busy or entertained, he was also being rewarded for good behaviour, all the while making him feel he is in control.

Positive Reinforcement not only works well on all kinds of pets, it's especially effective on children, bosses, employees and even spouses! Of course, Neil is better at using it on me, than I am on him. He's got more patience and I've got a bit of a short wick.

Our whole life consists of trying to outwit the little fellow. It usually works, but often we pay a price for it. His 'step-up' is basically bomb proof but he has moments when he insists on staying put. Pickles likes to be involved in the supper making process. Even if he's hungry, he won't always step up to go home (his cage) for supper because he likes to watch the pond and birdies from the dining room. If I suspect he's not in the mood to leave, instead of asking, "Wanna go home for supper?" I say, "Wanna help mommy make your supper?" and he'll trip

56

over his own feet in haste to get on my hand. Now, this is a good plan to get him home, but a major pain in the ass in the meantime.

To get his supper ready, I have to take a row of birdie bread out of the freezer, unwrap it to get a square, wrap it back up and put it back in the freezer – all this one-handed while Pickles perches on the other. All the while, Pickles is reaching for everything in the freezer and trying to rip the food out of my hand or trying to help remove the saran wrap.

I put the square in a small bowl and walk across the kitchen to the microwave, which is in a little pantry. While we wait a few seconds for it to warm up, Pickles is loosing his balance on my hand from trying to reach for shiny objects on the shelves and usually ending up upside-down. I can't place him on the counter yet, because I can't trust him alone for a second while I'm doing the other things but once the supper is ready, I set him down while I break up the square, stir in the Hemp Seed and put it into his cage bowl. While I'm trying to do this, Pickles is trying to get at his food before it's ready, running for the soggy dishcloth, inspecting the soap container, sprinting for the sugar bowl and tossing the cage bowl on the floor – all at once. He's just a little grey blur who's harder to catch than a mouse.

He loves the little jar of Hemp Seed and one day, manages to rip the lid out of my hand. He made a mad dash for it and grabbed it so fast that he was shocked he actually got it and his beak hadn't been prepared to hang on to it. The lid went flying, my hand flew after it and Pickles was determined to beat me to it. Nobody got it before it landed in a soap filled pan in the sink. Pickles had a full head of steam so by the time he stood on the brakes he had too much momentum. He slid feet first into the sink, grabbed on to the rim of the pan and flipped head first into the soapy water.

Soap and water were flying through the air as Pickles flapped his way out. Now he's livid and he takes it out on everything in sight. Both dishes go flying and as I bend over to pick up the bowls and the spilled food, Pickles managed to drop the wet dishcloth smack dab on my head. I came up in slow motion, giving him the evil eye as he snickered uncontrollably. When he finally stopped laughing, he asked, "Arncha hungry?"

Pickles definitely understands what's funny and he has a sick sense of humour. He has 3 laughs – one is an evil snicker, one is a nose laugh and the other, a chuckle – and most times they are accompanied by head bobs. He likes to tease, and he likes to play practical jokes. He hates to be teased himself, but is sometimes good-natured about being the butt of a practical joke. The guy is warped.

Most African Greys are known to be fearful of change and fearful of new items. Pickles is actually pretty good but when you least expect it, he freaks out. Changing furniture around can be scary for Greys and they like things just they way they are, thank you very much, but Pickles doesn't care a rat's ass what you do with furniture. We can usually bring a new sofa in the living room, a big scary item, but hand Pickles a nail file and he screams bloody murder.

He understands the word 'scary' and will tell us when something is scary to him. But he also likes to *pretend* that things are scary – screaming and flapping his wings in mock terror – he thinks that's hilarious.

Fortunately, loud noises don't bother him. Sudden noises – bad, loud noises - good. The first time we ever had a thunderstorm (and we get them a lot) I jumped up going "Woo hoooooooo!" and danced around until Pickles decided, what fun! One time, a thunderclap hit with no warning and Pickles was so startled, he fell part way off his perch but while hanging upside down, he shouted "Woo hoo!"

As far as change goes, he demands his supper on time and he demands to go to bed at the same time each night. Supper should be served at 5:00pm precisely, bedtime is 6:30pm and if he doesn't get his beauty sleep, he's a very cranky boy the next day. After we cover him he doesn't usually go to sleep right away, he prefers to hang out and eat some pellets, play with some talon toys and read a book. Okay, I'm sure he doesn't have a book under the covers but he will drone on and on with his words as if he's reading out loud. I think mainly, he wants to be locked in his cage and covered for some alone time. He probably figures it's us that are locked out and behind covers, not him.

But when it gets right down to it, all the food, toys and freedom, still isn't good enough. Pickles gets tired of some of his favourite foods sometimes, or maybe they're not in season or just not a good product so we're always looking for tasty new items. He has hundreds of toys but will tire of some quickly so we are constantly rotating. Sometimes just moving a toy to a new spot makes it more interesting but sometimes we need to put it away for a few weeks or months and when we bring it back out, he's thrilled with the 'new' toy. All the freedom outside the cage isn't good enough if he doesn't have enrichment or attention.

Learning about parrots and learning how to adapt to them is an on-going process, a lot of work and every day there is a new challenge. There is no other pet in the world that requires as much work, attention and patience as a parrot does. On the other hand, there is nothing more rewarding than a happy parrot.

Chapter 5

Working & Living at the RV Park

A couple of years after getting Pickles, we got out of the fly shop. We had owned and operated it for 10 years and it was time to move on to something else. An opportunity arose for us to operate the RV Park, part of the Wildlife Park in Kamloops so we took the job for one season – from April until mid September.

We were provided with an RV, large enough to provide an area for Pickles. We set up a smaller cage, a new play stand, a bunch of toys and a boing (a coiled wire, wrapped with rope for climbing and swinging). The entire RV Park could be seen through the windows, so this provided all kinds of activity and entertainment for Pickles. He could watch us working outside or coming and going to the registration office/convenience store so Pickles was quite happy with his new digs.

We took a tour of the Wildlife Park the first chance we got. It's amazing with all the animals and birds, and we even took in a Raptor's show. Vultures, owls, hawks and eagles were paraded one at a time and some flew through the audience on recall. All the animals, with the exception of the Peacocks, were indigenous to the area and were provided good habitat and lots of room to live out their days, as all had been rescued and unable to be rehabbed back to the wild.

There were a lot of birds hanging around the RV Park, many we were unfamiliar with because of the difference in elevation. Crows were in abundance so Pickles was in his glory talking to each and every one. Now and then the Peacocks would escape and they were beautiful in the RV Park surroundings. The campers were thrilled to see them but during their mating period, we had to watch the kids for fear these big aggressive birds would hurt them.

Pickles learned many, many more bird songs and he was happy to share the songs with all the people in the Park. Most visitors were not aware of Pickles and some were confused about the bird sounds coming from our corner of the grounds. Pickles would do his Nuthatch impression and people would look around for the bird. Their eyes would look skyward at the screeching of the hawk and we were asked if a lake is hidden in the woods after the haunting sound of a loon fills the evening air. Pickles began to answer the Peacocks' mating songs and I had to wonder if that's why they were escaping - in search of this new, potential mate.

Across the river, along the valley bottom, there are cattle grazing and bellowing. Pickles learned to moo, which was quite embarrassing when we'd go for our evening walks through the RV Park, with Pickles in his backpack. He'd moo the whole way and of course, him being in back, it appeared as if we were the cows.

Once again, Pickles became a draw for customers. He had a play stand in the store, he went for walks, got to socialize and everyone was fascinated with him. Soon, new customers were arriving and having heard about Pickles through the RV grapevine, had decided to make a stop on the way to their destination.

Pickles isn't very talkative while in his backpack outdoors, preferring to caw at the crows, sing to the birds and mumble like a little old man to himself so that you can only catch the odd word. When curious people approach us, it's sometimes difficult to get him to speak, he usually just laughs at them. One night, we were cornered by a group of children who kept asking Pickles to talk. "Speak Pickles, speak!" they all chimed. Eventually, Pickles responded with a deep "Woof!" The kids thought this was hilarious and tried to get him to do it again. "Speak Pickles! Bark! Speak!" until Pickles ordered them all to "Go home!"

61

Sometimes people want to hold him and Pickles is willing to sit on anybody's hand but we're careful who we allow contact with because sometimes he will run up an arm to the shoulder. If we think people can deal with this and not freak out, we'll hand Pickles off to them. We don't usually allow Pickles on our shoulders because sometimes he refuses to leave and it's too easy to get a nipped ear if he's irked, or he will hide right between your shoulder blades, where you can't reach him.

All too often, for some reason, people like to poke their fingers in his face. Are people really that retarded? One time, I set Pickles and the backpack down on a picnic table to chat with a couple of women. One of the women started to poke her finger through the bars and I told her that he doesn't like fingers in his face and won't hesitate to bite. She couldn't resist and while my back was turned, she went for it. I turned around just in time to see Pickles with a firm hold of the tip of her finger. His eyes glazed over in ecstasy as he held on tight and began to grind. Anybody who owns a bird from the parrot family knows how painful the beak grind can be, and Pickles was giving his all. I watched in horror as blood appeared and started to pool on the bottom of the cage.

The woman pretended it was no big deal as I banged on the cage, desperately trying to unbalance Pickles but all that did was make him grab on harder as he flapped for balance. Crap. The woman was about to drop to her knees in agony but she maintained her composure as I worked at getting her loose. Finally, I poked my finger next to hers and Pickles went for the new meat just as I yanked my finger back. "SCORE!!" he announced, through a bloody beak.

I turned to inspect the idiot woman's finger. She had quite the wound but still maintained that it wasn't a big deal. "It doesn't hurt" she said, through clenched teeth. Tears were forming but she insisted, "I'm okay."

Just then, Neil joined us and I told him what happened. It was obvious what he was thinking … "What kind of hair-brain DOES that?!" but all he managed was "Huh." He then asked me to come with him and he showed me a nestling crow, lying beneath a 30- foot pine tree. He looked basically full-grown and at first we thought he was, and that he'd been injured. All he could do was lie on his side, mouth gaping, and shuffle his feet in the dirt in an attempt to get away from us.

I knew there were 2 nests above, because I walked past this tree often and had been watching the baby crows in their various maturing stages. The nests weren't very high, just feet above my head. I glanced up and there were no other babies left, just adult crows cawing and dive-bombing us in protection of their young one. We weren't sure what to do but in the meantime I went and got some water soaked bread in case he was hungry or thirsty.

It was difficult to get the bread in his beak, even though his mouth was open. If we did, the crow wouldn't swallow it. Neil went for pliers and we fed him with that - like the beak of an adult, feeding it's young by getting it deep. By getting the food to the back of his throat, he was able to swallow. He was obviously hungry or thirsty, and he took quite a bit.

We decided he should be placed back in the nest, but which one? Neil got a long stick, fashioned a bucket to it, raised the crow to the lowest nest and tipped him in. I don't know if we placed him in the wrong nest and some adults threw him out, or if he fell out on his own, but the next morning he was back on the ground. Perhaps there was something wrong with him. The other babies had already flown the coop, maybe there was something wrong with his legs and he couldn't stand in preparation for flight. Maybe he was weak and the parents had rejected him and thrown him from the nest but then, why were they dive-bombing us?

We decided to let nature take its course and left him on the ground. I had taken another job and had to leave for the day but I received a call at work – Neil was concerned. The weather had reached 40 celsius, the crow was in the sun all day and he was afraid a kid or a dog would get at him. He wanted to bring the crow to the RV and put him in Pickles outdoor cage, beneath the canopy for protection until we found the proper authorities to take him. I agreed, even though that meant Pickles wouldn't be able to go outside for a while, and that the cage would need a good bleaching afterwards.

Neil wrapped the crow in a towel and carried him off with a half dozen crows following in frenzy. They perched in the trees next to the RV and complained all day while Neil went on with his work outside. In the meantime, I spent some time at work researching crows and looking for phone numbers of people to call and Neil spoke with the head guy at the WildLife Park. I couldn't find any place in the Kamloops area that would take a injured crow, even the Wildlife Park. They said they don't do crows, and that it wasn't a good idea to rehabilitate them back to the wild because they become too friendly, harass people for food in the Park Café, or get so friendly that someone takes them home for a pet. To boot, I found out that it's illegal for us to be in possession of a wild crow. I called the Ministry of Environment and explained the situation. They didn't know who would take a crow but I was given permission to take care of him until we could release him.

In the end, we had no choice but to nurse him until he was strong enough to fly. We just couldn't bring ourselves to leave him in the elements to die, even though nature should take care of it. To us, it wasn't 'nature' in an RV Park packed with people and dogs. He wouldn't stand a chance. We named him Parker, after the RV 'Park" and took on the parental obligations.

He was placed in the cage on the deck, beneath the awning and against the outer wall. On the other side of the wall, was Pickles' cage and play stand. Pickles couldn't see Parker, but he could hear him. The two of them cawed back and forth to each other, or at least Pickles would answer Parker's caws each time.

The first 3 or 4 days, Parker just lay on his side on the bottom of the cage on a bed of towels. We continued to feed him with pliers because it made it easier and because he should never be conditioned to human hands. We never pet him, or held him, and even tried to keep talking to a minimum. As a result, Parker never did learn to like us, or trust us.

We tried a variety of foods and he ate most readily - soppy bread, wieners, potatoes, fruit and veggies, worms and bugs – but I think his favorite was the dry dog food, which was loaded with protein. The WildLife guy told us that bread held no nutrition for him but it's the only way we could get water in him, he was too young to drink from a bowl. We were afraid to use a dropper as young crows can swallow wrongly and end up choking, so the wet bread got the water down.

By now, we knew the difference between a nestling and a fledgling. Nestlings can't fly and belong in the nest, fledglings leave the nest and spend days on the ground, under the careful eye of the parents, while learning how to fly. Often people try to rescue them, thinking they are abandoned or injured. Parker was a nestling who wouldn't be able to take care himself and the parents wouldn't be able to protect him.

Eventually, he was attempting to stand up but still wasn't able to perch on a cage branch. The cage wouldn't support his wingspan so we built a screened enclosure on the ground and filled one side with a pile of branches so that when he was ready, he could perch on them.

His parents, and the extended family, still hung around in the trees above to keep an eye on him and they constantly crowed their displeasure with us. I had read that youngsters of previous years would stay with their parents, helping them raise subsequent batches, or clutches, of babies. Our days were filled with the cacophony of crows, including Pickles.

As Parker got better at standing, we would release him from the cage for short periods of time. The first time we did, he tried to bolt but he was like a little drunken soldier who could only stagger round and round in circles, falling now and then on his side. He was eventually able to fly in short bursts until finally, he was able to land in a tree. He spent the first night there and the next day was able to fly a couple of hundred feet. We got busy at the park and when we returned, there was no sign of him. He'd flown the coop.

He had never learned to trust us and whenever we appeared, he would try to move away from us. After he flew away, he wasn't interested in returning for food or companionship; he just wanted the hell out of there. After that, we would catch sightings of him. We knew it was he because he was smaller than the rest in the group and his caw had always sounded more like a duck quack. He also drank from puddles better than the other juvenile crows he hung with, having to learn a little quicker in captivity.

We've always wondered how he faired and we now pay closer attention to all crows. I've always loved them, and like a stupid teenager, I once captured a friendly crow and kept him in the basement. Somebody had given me a large monkey cage (no idea why they had one) but mostly one of us kids would free him to fly around and interact with us. He was friendly, affectionate and fun but he sure made a mess of the basement. My mom eventually talked me into freeing him by making me feel guilty about taming a wild bird, that he needed to be with other crows and free to fly. But Parker had given me a new appreciation for these intelligent creatures that are loaded with personality.

Summer continued and it was a scorcher. The RV had air-conditioning and I stole back there every chance I got. One day I decided to take a nap while Neil was doing the weed whacking and just as I was dozing off, there came a knock at the door. I decided to ignore it but Pickles, the social butterfly, opts for answering the door. Pickles has 3 voices – mine, Neil's and his own – all sound naturally human.

Pickles: "Hello?"

Man: "Hello?"

Pickles: "Hellooooo!"

Man: "I need to check in, please."

Pickles: "We're out of beans!"

Man: "Excuse me?"

Pickles: "Fresh out of beans!"

Man: Silence.

Pickles: Silence.

Me: Dying a slow death.

Man: "Can I check in please?"

Pickles: "Well, hello there!"

Me, muttering under my breath: "For the love of God Pickles! Please, PLEASE, shut the hell UP!"

Man's wife join's Man …

Wife: "Isn't anybody home, honey?"

Pickles: "Everybody's home!"

Man: (very quietly) "I think there's a mentally handicapped person inside."

Me, to myself: "Oh great. Just great."

Pickles: (sings song) "Ring, ring, ring, ring, ring, ring, ring BANANA PHONE! Boop boop ba doop"

.

The sound of footsteps walking away.

Me: "Oh, thank God".

Pickles: Not yet finished and spotting them out the window lets go a loud wolf whistle and calls out "Bye-bye baby!"

It's over, they're gone, but I'm still cringing.

The next day I'm sitting outside the trailer (my long hair still in a bird's nest, raccoon eyes from last night's mascara, teeth still in a cup next to the bed) having my morning coffee as they go by, walking their dog. They spot me and suddenly pick up speed, heading away.

I'm tempted to yell out "I'm not crazy - I own a parrot!!!"

But, what's the use. It just...never...ends...

The office/store was only about 100 feet from our RV and some starlings had built a nest in the eaves. We enjoyed sitting on our deck, watching them. They were very busy, flying in and out to feed the babies. As the babies grew older (at least 8 of them), they'd appear at the opening, chirping and calling for their parents. One morning they all appeared on the roof outside, jumping up and down, testing their wings. Suddenly, they all took off in one fell swoop. Just like that, they had gone exploring only to return now and then for a few moments until they were gone for good.

The parents still hung around and we soon realized they had another batch of babies. More entertainment! But the store needed a new roof and we knew the contractors would be starting soon. We hoped the babies would have time to mature but it wasn't the case.

They showed up one morning while Neil was in town and I was preparing for the day. I went outside for my coffee and to see what would happen. Starlings are considered a nuisance around there, there's too many of them and I knew there was nothing that could be done for them but I wasn't prepared for what I saw.

When the crew ripped off the eaves, it was discovered that the nest went down into the outer walls. A guy was on a ladder, pulling out huge handful after handful of straw bedding while another guy was working next to him on the roof. The first guy came up with a baby dangling by the feet and in the blink of an eye, the other guy snipped off his head with a tool. I was horrified. And frozen in place. I wanted to yell at them but I knew it would do no good, they had a job to do, they couldn't stop for birds and the birds were too young to survive on their own. So, I said nothing. A minute later, the first guy came up with another baby but the other guy was further away and told him to just throw it on the roof, that the crows would eat it. I was dying inside.

The crew knocked off early, only an hour into the job, and took off in their trucks. I wanted to climb the ladder and look for the bird but I'm deathly afraid of heights so I just walked around the building looking for signs of the baby. Neil arrived while I was looking and I asked him to climb up and check the roof but he couldn't find the chick.

I went back to sit on the deck and suddenly, the two parent starlings appeared from behind the building, flapping and dancing half off the ground, with the baby running after them. The three of them ducked into a large bush and for the rest of the day, the parents were in and out tending to him. The next day I looked but never saw any sign of them from then on.

I was telling somebody about it later on and I found out that starlings are actually protected! I learned that construction comes to a standing halt where nests are concerned! Oh God, the guilt that set in. I was mortified that I had let this happen and I'll never forgive myself. After doing some research on starlings, I discovered they had great character and intelligence. They can actually learn to talk and I even watched a video of a talking pet starling. No need to chastise me, I continuously punish myself. I was wrong. Dead wrong.

Eventually the roof was completed. It was gabled so it was cooler in the store now and Pickles enjoyed hanging out with us, or playing with the hanging toys on his play stand. One particular day, he was in an especially playful and talkative mood. He bantered back and forth with us and any customers who visited.

Pickles is almost always eager to talk to people but the odd time, he sits like a lump and refuses to display the slightest hint of his talents. People scoff at our claims of a bird with over 100 words (at that time) in his vocabulary. No amount of prodding will make him speak up. It makes us feel a little bad because the excitement of meeting a real live, talking parrot quickly turns to disappointment for them when Pickles won't speak.

70

A young couple walked in with their son, a toddler. Pickles LOVES kids so he immediately swung down the branches to the base of the stand, as close as possible to the boy.

Pickles: Hello baby.

Boy: Stares in surprise.

Pickles: Wanna grape?

Boy: Mouth gapes, eyes widen.

Pickles: Dontcha wanna grape?

Boy: Grabs and hugs daddy's leg.

Pickles: Let's go getta grape. Dontcha wanna eacher grape? Wanna potato?

Boy: Lips begin to quiver.

Pickles: SPEAK.

Boy: WAAAAAAAAAAAAAAAAAAAAAAAAA

Pickles: WAAAAAAAAAAAAAAAAAAAAAAAAAAA

Mom and dad rush little boy out of store.

Pickles scurries up the branches to watch them leave through the window then tucks one foot up, fluffs up his feathers, puffs out his cheeks and mumbles "What a bean."

Ha! The shoe's on the other foot. Now he knows how it feels.

Now and then, people who had heard about Pickles but had never seen him would come to our RV in hopes of meeting him. We didn't really like people dropping by because we worked basically from sun up to sun down, always dealing with people and we sought privacy, whenever we could get it. But a nice couple showed up one evening as we were eating appetizers so we invited them in and shared some food after they finished admiring Pickles.

We sat down to chat and had two conversations going at one time. Suddenly I became aware of another voice. I turned to see Pickles, on a branch, reaching as close as possible to us, hollering "WANNA SPEAK! WANNA SPEAK! WANNA SPEAK!"

"Sorry Pickles. What did you wanna say?" I asked.

"I said hello," Pickles answered.

Everybody said "Hello" back.

Then Pickles informed the closest guest to him, "You got some on your beak".

"What's on my beak?" the guest asked.

"Piiiizzzzzaaaaaa" (pizza) informed Pickles, and then added, "Wanna eat something to eat?"

Our stint at the RV Park was almost at an end and I had been thinking about getting a dog. I searched around for a Doberman Rescue and found one in a nearby town. One thing led to the next and a couple of days before we packed up, I came home with a large, red Dobie. He was about 4 years old and appeared as laid back as the 2 Dobies I had owned in previous years. I brought him, on a short leash, to introduce him to the bird but he immediately lunged for Pickles. I thought, hmmmm, maybe he's just excited to see him and just wanted to sniff at Pickles. When I had first brought a kitten home to another Doberman I had owned, this dog had lunged at the kitten but only to sniff, lick and play. It had scared me at first but that dog was nothing but gentle and caring with that kitten from the moment they met.

I held on tight to the leash and slowly brought the dog's head closer to Pickles but his mouth opened and his teeth snapped. That was it, back to the rescue centre. I was sad – he was a nice dog and deserved a good home, but this wasn't the one for him. I would look for another dog.

Our time at the Park had been good for Neil and Pickles. Before the Park, their relationship had been improving day by day but over the summer, their bonding became complete. I wasn't around that much, having taken a full time job in Kamloops, so the two of them spent a lot of time together. Neil stopped into the RV often throughout the day to give Pickles snacks or to play with him. The rest of the time, Pickles could watch Neil from the windows as he went about his day. Neil could hear Pickles chattering and singing from just about anywhere in the park and from time to time Pickles would call out "Daddy home?" Neil call back "Pretty soon" and Pickles would holler, "Woo hoo!" and go back to whatever he was doing. It must have looked and sounded pretty strange to anyone watching.

When I was home, and we were all in the RV, Pickles would become antsy. Nothing would please him – snacks, games, attention – he was miserable and we didn't know how to make him happy. At times, we couldn't stand his demanding

73

screeches so we'd tell him 'bye-bye' and go sit out on the deck. The minute we said 'good bye' he would perk right up and hoot, holler and whistle. He could hear us on the other side of the wall, he knew we were there, and yet he continued with his happy sounds the whole time. To this day, Pickles does the same thing any time we leave the house.

It was at the Park where Neil started taking Pickles on "Snack Safaris". When Pickles wasn't looking, Neil would hide the small bowl of pine nuts. Pickles would step up on his hand while they went looking through rooms, closets, and cupboards until they found the bowl. Pickles loves this game. He will show Neil where to look by leaning so far out in the direction he wants to go, that he almost falls off his hand. Each time that the pine nuts aren't in the spot Pickles chose, he'd fluff up in disappointment and go "hmmmm" but quickly lean towards the next spot until finally the bowl is discovered and he blurts, "THERE'S the snacks!" He's then rewarded with the opportunity to eat as many as he likes from the bowl.

Our last day at the RV Park, a man came in to the office to talk to me. I had warned Neil several times, "If you are going to put an RV next to ours, make sure you warn the people. Tell them about Pickles and all the noise he makes at 6:00 in the morning when we get up." Does he listen? No.

The man asks if I have a parrot. "Why yes I do!" I replied, all proud like. "That's what I thought," Grumbled the guy, "Sure wish you would have warned us." "Huh?" I said, suddenly feeling not so proud.

Turns out the wife had a bad dream that morning. Something about an alien invasion in the RV Park. Why? Because Pickles' vocal menu this morning included cel phones, sirens, whistles, ray guns and the beep beep beep of vehicles backing up.

74

When the wife woke up, but still half asleep, she was horrified to find the chaotic sounds were coming from right outside her window. Believing that we were in a state of emergency almost gave the old gal a coronary.

They were NOT happy campers. No sense of humour.

Next time I saw Pickles, I gave him a piece of my mind. Told him he was a brat and that he shouldn't upset poor old people like that. Told him he got me in trouble – AGAIN.

Pickles was on his play stand and lumbered up slowly and thoughtfully, as close as possible to me. His stance and facial expression projected deep thought and wisdom as he stared deep into my eyes and profoundly replied, "Eat your beak."

On that note, we left the RV Park and headed back home.

Chapter 6

Pickles Gets a Dog

It was the end of September; we were finally home and settling in for the winter. Winters can be long and harsh in this high altitude town and I despise it. The snow can be beautiful and I love the silence it brings with it, and the sparkling clean look of trees laden with snow but once Christmas passes, I have absolutely no use for it. Winter brings blubber. Blubber's supposed to be gained *before* winter, for warmth and sustenance but I stack on the pounds *during* winter. We don't participate in winter sports; we just eat for lack of anything better to do. I get bored and when I get bored, I'm miserable. Poor Neil, I think it's akin to throwing a bear in the cabin and locking the doors. How that sweet, good-natured guy puts up with me, I'll never know.

I figure, let's get a dog. He would be good company, we could walk him for exercise and keep in shape. Yeah! That's the ticket! So, I contacted the Doberman Rescue centre again and within a couple of days, we bonded with a sweet little black and tan Dobie named Athena. She was good-natured and laid back, so laid back that mostly she slept. She had lived in 4 homes by the time she was 3, never abused but mostly neglected. We were assured that she was not aggressive and it seemed her only baggage was separation anxiety and fear of abandonment. Perfectly understandable.

We brought her home and took her to meet Pickles. Poor thing. She had no idea that she was about to become Pickles personal plaything, or the equivalent of the tormented little brother. We entered the living room and Pickles went ballistic! He booted it, half running, half flying, tripping over himself and falling off branches in his haste to get close to her. Between flutters and tumbles, he cried out "Hello baby! Well hello there! Wanna scratch? Wanna potato? Helllooooo!" Once to the bottom of his stand and close to Athena, he couldn't keep his eyes of her. He talked and laughed, talked and laughed and kept it up for hours.

Except for all the commotion when entering the room, Athena barely looked at Pickles, she couldn't care less. She stayed that way and has never been a threat to him. We weren't stupid though – animals will be animals and we were careful never to set them up for disaster.

The day after we got her, we all went to the yard first thing in the morning for a spectacular, warm autumn's day. Pickles was in his aviary and Athena settled in the grass to gnaw on a bone while we sipped our coffee. We sat next to the aviary, admiring nature and marvelling at our happy new family.

Pickles was still infatuated with Athena and did his very best to get her attention, stopping only long enough to heckle neighbours and passer-bys. Athena finally heads in Pickles' direction so Pickles comes lower and closer to the aviary screen. Athena squats to pee and Pickles cries out "Water! Gurgle gurgle. Fresh water!" This is simply amazing to Pickles. He's doing circles and head bobs and shouting "Fresh Water! Fresh Water!".

At some point, Athena spots a passing dog and won't stop barking at the intruder. Pickles is startled by the first loud bark, loses his balance, flips upside down on his branch and hangs there like a stunned bat. He regains his senses but remains upside down, beating his wings and emitting that bone chilling African Grey scream. Once upright, Pickles hollers to Athena "Stop it! Just stop it!" and like a good dog, she did!

Pickles settles down and sits all tucked up with his cute little puffy cheeks as Athena wanders next to him, squats and produces a big pile of diahrea poop. Pickles whips his head toward us as if to say "Did you see that!?" then looks back at the steaming pile and asks "Pudding?" As I'm wiping the coffee I just spit off the back of Neil's head, Pickles carried on, "Pudding?   Want pudding! Mmmmm".

The chilly autumn crept in and there were no more yard days after that. Neil is off work for the winter while I continue my job in Kamloops. If I could find a job that could support us both, I'd gladly work while Neil stayed home and played homemaker. He's good at it and enjoys both cooking, baking and cleaning. When I get home, the house is clean and supper's on the table. For desert, there's usually homemade cake, cookies, pie or something really fattening, and I don't have to do a damn thing. I, on the other hand, am a lousy wife and hate doing anything remotely wifely.

While I was at work one day, Neil was preparing dinner and I was expected home shortly. Neil's in the kitchen when he hears Pickles announce "Mamma's home." Athena leaps from the couch and runs to the window barking while Neil follows. They both stand at the window but there's no car in the driveway and Neil realizes he's been duped. Athena's still positive I am arriving – the bird said so – and she continues to bark while Pickles shouts "Stop it! Just stop it!" Athena's barking and Pickles is shouting until Neil settles everybody down and goes back to cooking dinner.

Moments later, Pickles hollers "Mamma's home!" Athena jumps up barking, Neil runs to the living room and both stand staring out the window. Psyche. Neil catches on but Athena can't believe a bird would lie so she keeps barking. "Go lay down!" Pickles demands. "Stop it! Go lay down!" Athena barks a couple of hesitant woofs then reluctantly goes back to the couch. Neil goes back to the kitchen.

"MAMMA'S HOME!!!!!!!" Pickles screams. Running … barking. Man and dog stare out the window. Bilked again. Neil is feeling pretty sheepish, Athena's not sure what to believe and now she's whining. Pickles whines right back at her, only he takes it up a few notches. Neil goes back to dinner, Athena lies down and stares at the bird confused and hurt.

"MAMMA'S HOME!!!!!!" Athena merely lifts her head as Neil rushes past her to the window. I guess it's true what they say about old dogs and new tricks.

Winter goes on, we get fatter as our plans for dog walking get blown out the window. There's always a reason – it's too cold, too much snow or too icy but mainly, it's because Athena hates the cold. Good choice eh? A hairless Doberman in a high altitude winter climate. We have a hard time walking on ice but Athena is worse. Dobies simply don't have the paws for grabbing, she's just slipping all over the place. But we get by and somehow, Athena remains slim, even with the lack of exercise.

Spring finally arrives and I'm able to take Athena for walks and runs. Her recall's not great and we work at it but I have to be careful about where I let her run. We were assured she had no aggression but soon find out she will go after other dogs. The moment she reached them, she would spin on her heels and head back but we were afraid she'd do that to the wrong dog some day and cause a fight.

Athena is still showing no interest in Pickles but just to be safe, we had erected a sturdy screen door between the living room and kitchen to separate bird and dog when we're not around. We were more afraid of Pickles approaching Athena, than the other way around. Pickles is a little bugger and he could saunter over and nip Athena, given half a chance.

Neil goes back to work in spring and this year he's managing Lac Le Jeune Provincial Park. I left my job in Kamloops and went to work as the gatekeeper in the same park. There are 144 campsites in the park and it's situated on a lake with excellent trout fishing. Wildlife is plentiful, including deer, moose and the odd black bear.

Along the lakeshore, there's a really nice day-use/picnic area and one day I was sent to write tickets for any vehicles without a parking pass. It was Canada Day, the beach was packed and the parking lot contained many violators so I got busy writing. As I approached a car, writing on my clipboard, I failed to notice a pothole and everyone around me heard the crack as I stepped into it and broke my ankle. As I was falling and trying to right myself, I sprained the other one. As I sat on the ground, unable to speak through the pain, many people came to assist but I wouldn't let them look because I hadn't shaved my legs. I spent the rest of the summer on cast and crutches. So much for walking the dog.

With a broken ankle, the simplest things became nearly impossible, like taking a shower. I had to wash my hair in the bathroom sink so I'd have something to lean against while my hands were busy. One day, I'm washing my hair while Athena lounges on the bed. The whole while, Pickles is chirping and whistling at the top of his lungs. "What a happy bird." I'm thinking, as I rinse my hair.

"Heyyyy, wait a minute" I think to myself, "He's a little *too* loud" and I turn off the water to hear him better. He sounds closer than the living room so I wrapped my head in a towel and hobbled to the living room to check it out.

No bird. He's not on the top of the cage where I left him, he's not in the usual 'fly down' places and of course, he shut the heck up now. I know how he loves this

80

game so I'm off on the hunt once again, knowing full well he's sitting coyly, head bobbing and watching my every move. I always feel so silly playing this game, knowing that a little smart ass bird is fully aware of the fact that he's pulling one over on me.

Not on the couch. Not on his living room play stand. Not on a lampshade. The living room is void of birds.

Not in the bowl of fruit on the kitchen counter or typing at the keyboard.

On to the dining room but not on his play stand, table or hutch.

As I turn to leave the dining room, Pickles just can't contain himself any longer. He snickers. I scan the room again but he's invisible. Another snicker, I narrow it down from the sound. "Pickles?" I call. He answers with a cough and a sneeze. Aha! Under the kitchen table.

I bend down to look and there he is, crouching on a chair seat, poised to flee. "Ack!" he shouts as I reach for him, but I'm not fast or nimble enough, restricted by my crutches, and he launches – straight into the sliding window door. He goes down in a crumpled heap, shakes it off and attempts to escape through the glass again. I head over to retrieve him but he doesn't like the crutches, especially from his floor level. Over and over he leaps and slams into the glass, all the while crying "Aviary? Aviary? Aviary?" which he sees within reach, if it weren't for this stupid window between them.

I'm trying to maneuver crutches and bend over to nab him before he hurts himself but it's a difficult task and I end up toppling into an armchair. Pickles spots an opportunity to head for the hills and he sprints, running low with his wings splayed for balance. But there's an obstacle – Athena appears before him,

81

attracted by all the excitement. Pickles pauses momentarily, assesses his blocked escape route and opts to go for it anyway and shoots between Athena's legs.

Athena is mortified as the little grey plane taxies at full break speed towards her. She starts to hop like a cat on a hot tin roof, trying to keep her feet out of beak reach but trying not to hurt Pickles at the same time. This confuses Pickles and he's trying to get out from under but everywhere he heads, paws are raining down around him.

So there in the middle of the floor is a dancing, hopping, circling dog with a trapped, dancing, hopping, circling bird crying "oh oh oh oh oh oh oh oh."

Finally I reach the commotion and scoop Pickles up. Pickles is livid and demands "Wanna go home!" so I plop him down on the base edge of his play stand where he promptly turns his back on me and sits muttering to himself.

Athena follows meekly, slightly traumatized by the whole ordeal and worried that she may have been the bad one. She appears to be concerned about Pickles and gingerly sniffs and inspects him from a safe distance. Pickles is angry with me but turns to Athena and asks sweetly "Wanna snackery kiss?" What a suck up.

The two of them got along well. Even though Pickles constantly teased and tormented Athena, he really liked her company and spent a lot of time trying to interact with her. Athena would lie sleeping on the floor beneath the play stand and Pickles would perch above, talking a mile a minute. He'd tell her stories, ask her questions and if possible, poop on her. He'd specifically move around the bottom of the play stand to position himself above her, let one go and bob his head madly when he scored. Athena totally ignored Pickles, except to obey the odd command to "go lay down". And of course, Pickles yelled out "Mamma's home!" any time he was bored, just to watch her run to the window barking. He'd wait until she settled down, rolled up in a ball on her bed and do it again. That dog - never once did she suspect it might be a lie.

My ankle never did heal properly (even 3 years later) and it was difficult to walk Athena. Neil worked on his feet, almost every day and sometimes 10 to 12 hours so I couldn't expect him to always be walking her but sometimes he did. She was becoming more and more aggressive towards other dogs and I could hardly hold her back. I couldn't plant my feet because of my ankle and it was getting embarrassing, not being able to control my own dog.

Her barking had become constant. She'd go to the yard and just stand there barking at something that seemed visible only to her. We got it under control for a while by rewarding her with a cookie every time she was quiet, telling her "Good girl, no bark!" But I think because I couldn't walk her, she was getting bored. I would still take her places to let her run loose but now winter had arrived again. I needed help.

We worked with behaviorists and I tried any advice I could get. Nothing seemed to work and I was frustrated because I'd never owned, or dealt with, an aggressive dog before. I applied all the Positive Reinforcement techniques that are used for parrot training but nothing seemed to work with Athena. I was at a loss, and it was getting worse.

She nipped at a guy's butt once, which shocked me because until that time, Athena was only dog aggressive. As I was getting out of the car one day, I opened the back door to get my groceries and Athena, spying a small dog, bolted from the car. Before I could react, she had the little dog pinned to the ground with her jaws at the belly. Fortunately, I was able to call her off and the little dog ran away. I spoke with the owner later, who had seen it happen from down the street, and he said his dog bore no marks. But that was it. I had to let her go.

83

I had to give her up, for her own good. I felt her aggression had been misrepresented to me and thought it irresponsible and unfair to her, but perhaps she hadn't been at the rescue center long enough for them to properly assess her. In the meantime (1 ½ years), we had bonded and it was hard to let go but she needed someone who had experience in dealing with aggressive dogs, or a home with acreage to run. I've owned dogs, always from pups, all my life but I was at a loss with this one. I cried all the way to, and back from, the rescue center. I had failed her.

We let her go in the spring and it was a sad house for a long time. Pickles would call for her but Athena never appeared. We all missed her and as the summer passed, we felt we needed to fill that void so in August, I went looking for another dog. I wanted a small dog this time, and one that I could control on walks. We settled on a Min Pin (Miniature Pinscher, but no relation to the Doberman) and found the cutest little rust colored, 8 week old puppy. I spoke with my First Nations friend and asked him for a name that meant sweet or gentle and he immediately came up with 'Neeka', which means 'Darling One'. He's very spiritual and believes a name can shape the character.

We brought the little guy home and introduced him to Pickles. Pickles is thrilled because dogs are chumps, they are easily deceived and he has a brand new victim. Neeka was doomed to spend his life as the butt of all Pickles' practical jokes.

Neeka is just teensy weensy. So tiny that a finger is almost too big to pet his head and his belly can't be stroked without making contact with his little dick. Correction - he has a *huge* dick for such a little pup, embarrassingly large. And he loves his dick. He checks with it about everything. If he gets in trouble, he immediately pokes his dick as if it were to blame. Get away from the cage Neeka, poke the dick. Leave that remote alone Neeka, poke the dick. Neil says he's whispering to his dick, like Brick on the TV show "The Middle" and thinks they're plotting together. Neeka tried to copulate with everything in sight and

84

stuffed toys didn't stand a chance. He always had an erection and couldn't walk because it would rub on his chest and make him friskier. We got him neutered but it was as if it didn't take. It took 2 years for his obsession to fade, and for the erections to *mostly* go away but he still blames his dick for all his troubles.

Neeka learned real fast that there's food under Pickles' area and Pickles knows that Neeka's not supposed to scrounge for it but Pickles can't resist enticing him. One time, Neeka was sitting on the floor, a couple of feet from where Pickles was sitting on the edge of the play stand and eating white pith from the inside of a piece of orange peel. He finished but Neeka wasn't looking at him so he leaned out as far as he could reach, rolling the peel around on his tongue without taking his eyes of the dog. Neeka happened to glance up and Pickles promptly dropped the rind on the floor. A quick remand from Neil stops Neeka in his tracks. Pickles chuckles because he's just found a new game and there's no shortage of food to play with.

Neeka is a little confused about who gives the orders around here – us, or the talking bird. Pickles is the bossiest and most demanding so Neeka probably feels that Pickles is the alpha person in the house. Pickles takes every opportunity to keep the chain of command in tact. He will slide down the outside corner of his cage and call Neeka. He thinks that if he whispers, even though I'm right there, that I can't see or hear him. He whispers "Neeka. Neeka. Neeka come." Little kissy noises to call the dog. "Neeka." Neeka obeys and heads toward him but Pickles immediately reprimands him with a shout, "NO BIRD!!"

Pickles antagonizes Neeka by learning all the squeaky toys and making the squeaky sounds when Neeka's out of the room. Neeka races in to the room in hopes of catching the toy thief but he never catches on because Pickles pretends to be sleeping.

I swear that bird sits and plots the majority of his day and it's a good thing that Neeka is so good-natured and able to put up with it because it keeps Pickles from focusing his evil on us.

Neeka turned out to be the sweetest little dog. He's playful, cuddly, smart and loaded with character. A bit of a mommy suck but I like it that way. He's attentive to Pickles, but in a good way. Neeka watches Pickles play, obeys some of his commands and always watches for food to drop. Pickles watches Neeka a lot too and likes to chat it up with him. I don't let the two of them get too close though because Pickles might nip him and, even though Neeka would never bite on purpose, it's possible he could bite out of surprise and injure Pickles. We still have the screen door protecting Pickles in the living room for times we're busy or gone from the house. Neeka's good on a leash, never pulls, and he has great recall when off leash.

He's absolutely perfect, except he gets a little upset when we leave without him, but don't most dogs? What a contrast between Pickles and Neeka. If we leave the house, Neeka barks and howls, Pickles whistles and hoots at the top of his lungs. Neeka's upset, Pickles is happy.

While preparing to leave the house one day, Neeka frets and Pickles is practically pushing us out the door calling "Go bye-bye. Be gone long time".

Neeka screams bloody murder as we shut the door, walk to the car and drive away - Pickles sings at the top of his lungs, "Doodle-oodle-oo, woo hoo, doodle-oodle-oo!"

Neeka dashes out the doggy door and runs along the fence line, barking at the car as it drives away – Pickles caws like a crow in the background.

Neeka is absolutely positive we are going off to find some nice trail to walk. He knows darn well we're going to throw sticks, give each other cookies for coming when called and all kinds of other good stuff – Pickles could care less where we're going, just be back for supper.

In the end, they're both thrilled when we get home …

Neeka gets so excited he pees a little - Pickles drops a load.

Neeka squeaks with glee – Pickles announces "Daddy Bird's home! Everybirdy's home!"

Neeka scampers around our feet, looking for attention - Pickles demands "Supper! Want some supper! Dontcha want some supper? Wanna eat some supper with your beak? Let's go get some supper! Aren't ya hungry? Step up, let's go! Let's go, let's go, let's go!"

Once settled in the living room, Neeka steals a lap – Pickles sits on the edge of the couch and asks "Wanna party in your beak?"

Neeka's a happy little dog. At 2 years old, he is only 6 pounds and slim. He loves the yard and spends hours hanging around under brush, chasing his beach ball or laying in the sun. Pickles likes it when I play fetch with Neeka and throw the plastic bone over the aviary. He flaps and screams himself into a frenzy, laughing and falling upside down. He calls Neeka if he takes too long bringing it back and reprimands him as he runs past on his return.

Pickles has never shown any sort of jealousy toward Neeka. We can cuddle Neeka, feed him or play with him and Pickles doesn't care a lick. He's not jealous when Neil and I hug either, as some birds can be.

Pickles and Neeka are completely opposite in nature. Pickles is outgoing and brash while Neeka is shy and aims to please. Neeka is a ray of sunshine while Pickles is like some malevolent force of nature. They like each other, they amuse each other and they're content in their weird bi-polar relationship.

Chapter 7

Our Home Life

Everybody exists well in our household. If we're not spending time all together or paired off with somebody, everyone's happy to entertain themselves for the most part but Pickles needs the most attention. A quick walk around the house, transportation to another room for a change of scenery or a short conversation is all it usually takes to please him. When we walk him, he perches on our hand while doing the 'Grey Lean' to indicate to us where he wants to go and it's usually the chest freezer in the laundry room. This is a good surface to flat-foot around and make cool banging noises with his beak. Flat-footing parrots always make me laugh and Pickles is no exception. He doesn't have a lot of control on this slippery surface and once he gets going, it's sometimes hard to stop at the edge so he's like a little airplane suddenly presented with the end of a runway. Or he'll stand flat-footed while banging the freezer and each bang causes a slight slip so he bangs and slips around the whole surface.

After he's through banging, he likes to feel the freezer vibrations. He puffs up in a squatting position and his eyes glaze over, as the vibrations possess his body. I'm not sure if this is sensual for him, or just soothing but he will sit for long periods of time like this. Once out of his daze, he pushes his beak along the surface like a little snowplow and honks like a goose, then he wants to step up and get on to the next destination. He has to be taken to each room in the house, look out each window and dance in front of the bathroom mirror. It's at this point that he's trained to poop in the bathroom sink and if I position him right, he's able to drop his load right down the drain. A bull's-eye is accompanied by happy little head bobs.

The last stop after a walk has to be the dining room to play on his boings. The dining room set-up changes from month to month. Sometimes it's just ropes and boings, sometimes a play stand with toys, maybe his cat scratch post with box to climb around in or sometimes just a smaller cage. He likes the living room set-up to stay the same but he gets bored with things quickly in the dining room.

On one occasion, after dropping him off on his boings, Neil came home from work smelling of smoke and gasoline from burning slash piles at the park and headed straight to the shower. Pickles usually goes with him but Neil didn't want to subject him to the smell of gas so he went without him.

Pickles sat on his boing in the dining room, flustered that Daddy had ran in the house and straight past him with hardly a word.

"Daddy's home?" he asks in Neil's wake.

"Yes Pickles." I answer.

"Where Daddy?" he ponders.

I tell him Daddy's taking a shower.

"WATER??" he demands.

I tell him yes so now he's indignant because he didn't get to go with Neil. But, (and suspiciously quickly) he gives up the indignation and begins to swing in circles upside-down on his boing. At first he swings at a normal speed but then speeds up, faster and faster by beating his wings at the bottom of the boing. Suddenly, in all the commotion, he loses his footing and falls to the ground. This happens now and then and he's happy to be picked up and set back up. But this time, as I go to give him a hand up, he lifts his little foot as if to step up then suddenly darts overtop of my hand and makes a break for it. There's nowhere to go - in his haste he hadn't planned a very good escape route and I have him cornered. I attempt another 'step up' but he fakes to the left and runs past me to the right. I turn in time to see a flash of red tail disappear into the hallway.

When I appear at the head of the hall, he's frozen in place and a little grey face is cocked and staring up at me. He looks up at me, glances down the hallway, back up at me then sizes up the length of the hall to the bathroom and makes a break for it announcing "Bye Bye. Be right back."

Now, there's nothing funnier than a running, waddling, pigeon-toed Grey - especially when they're on the lam. I'm laughing by now as he's running to beat the band, hollering "Daddeeeeeeeeeeeee! Daddeeeeeeeeeeee!" - like I'm some kind of monster after him - glancing over his shoulder now and then, afraid that I may overtake him at any moment. Halfway down the hallway, I guess he's starting to panic that I'll nab him before he makes it to the bathroom so he starts alternating between running, hopping and flapping a few inches off the ground. Now I'm in stitches - and still at the head of the hall, not having gone anywhere near him.

I knew what he was thinking. He's obviously watched too many horror movies where the good guy is running from the monster, gets to his front door, fumbles with the keys and just as he's inserting the key and turning the doorknob, he turns his head just in time to see the jaws of death descending upon him.

Finally he arrives at the bathroom door, which has about a 2-inch gap from the floor. He hurls himself under it but gets no further than his shoulders. "DADDEEEEEEEEEE!!!!!" he screams from the floor. Neil finally hears all the

91

ruckus and peeks out from behind the shower curtain to find a bird wedged under the door, pleading eyes staring up at him. Neil's a little concerned and asks if he's okay but by then I've arrived at the door to rat him out so Neil ignores him and goes back to his shower.

Pickles backs up from the door, looks up at me then makes another dive for it - this time laying on his side, reaching under the door with one talon. No dice - can't fit. Now he has to face the music so he opts for sucking up. He cocks his head so that one eye is staring up sheepishly at me and asks sweetly "Wanna kiss?" then blows me one ... "mmmwha."

Well, how can I pretend to stay mad at that?? I blow a kiss back at him and he puts a foot up saying "Step up, let's go home." I oblige and carry him back to his boing.

Now he's pretty proud of himself for taking a little excursion with no dire consequences so he begins hooting and chirping as he starts swinging madly on his boing again. He's swinging and flapping upside down so wildly that he's banging into the wall and I tell him "Be careful Pickles!" to which he stops dead, still upside down, looking at me and asks "Is it scary?"

He rights himself, wiggles his bottom and poops. I had forgotten to put newspaper below him so I grabbed a Kleenex and knelt to clean it up.

"What's up?" He asks.

"I'm picking up poop." I answer.

He looks at me intently then asks "Baby butt poop?"

This made me laugh so of course Pickles joined in with his cackling and head bobs then breaks into song - his own rendition of Old MacDonald, Home on the Range and Knick Knack Patty Whack Give a Dog a Bone" but his version – I'll never forget it - went like this ... "Baby butt, baby butt, baby baby baby butt, baby butt, quack quack, knick knack, patty whack give a dog a hooooome, home on the range ...."

That bird really knows how to crack me up but I think he cracks himself up more.

Pickles loves his TV and it has to be on all the time or he gets cranky. I don't know that he really watches the screen, like some birds are known to do, but he definitely likes the noise. He picks up many different sounds from the television, mostly from commercials. He will sing, whistle or talk right along exactly as it's playing. He likes football and hockey and will shout, "SCORE!" if the crowd goes crazy. It's almost like he understands the meaning of this word because he always seems to use it appropriately. Such as the time I was cleaning his cage and he bonked the top of my head, yelled "Score!" and ran away chuckling.

Pickles is American Idol's biggest fan and is always in complete disagreement with Simon. The worse the singer, the more Pickles sings along – interjecting with "Whatta good song! Woo hoo!"

One evening, while Neil and I were watching TV, a commercial came on and I went to the kitchen to make a snack. Neil and I always let each other know when the program comes back on and before I finish making the snacks, I hear Neil say, "It's on." so I drop everything to go back to the couch, but the commercial's still on. I ask Neil why he called me back but he said he didn't. We look at Pickles. Can't be. I go back to the kitchen and seconds later I hear "It's on." I go back to find Neil shrugging and pointing accusingly at Pickles.

93

Since then, when Pickles announces a program is on, we have to warn the other "No it's not." And of course Pickles has picked up on that too so all we hear during commercials is him saying, "It's on. No it's not. It's on. No it's not." Luckily, Pickles had decided that commercials are what's really important so mostly he only announces "It's on" when the commercials start.

A typical evening around our house is watching TV and interacting with Pickles and Neeka. It's family time with pets instead of kids. This evening was fairly typical …

The phone rings as Pickles is dining on green beans. As it's ringing, Pickles is repeating the ringing in the bowl – which he discovers produces a really interesting echo. So while Neil answers the phone, Pickles continues the bowl ringing. He realizes the beans are impeding the good sounds so he tosses them out, one by one. But now he notices daddy is engrossed in a telephone conversation and wants in on the act.

He often carries on telephone conversations with himself and in between, he makes what must be the sound he hears of someone talking on the other end of the phone – kind of an electronic garbling. So while Neil is talking, Pickles' own conversation goes ... "Ring. Beep. Hello? (garble) What? (garble) mmmmm. (garble) Everybody's home. (garble) Huh? (garble) Wanna good story? (garble) Okay bye. Beep."

Pickles has put an end to his conversation and decides Daddy must be coached to do so too so he's telling Neil, "Okay bye. Beep. Okay bye. Beep. Okay BYE. Beep. OKAY BYE!!! Daddeeeeeeeeeee! Go BYE!!!!!!"

Neil finally tells his friend that Pickles has ordered him off the phone and hangs up. Neil tells Pickles what a brat he is while Pickles skips away, head bobbing and snickering. Neil goes after him saying, "Come here my little Chickadee." So

Pickles does the chickadee song, "Chicka dee dee dee" but it quickly changes to "Dad dee dee dee."

Neil asks Pickles if he's a Chickadee but Pickles explains that he is in fact a Big Eagle. He doesn't always do the usual raising of wings that other parrots do, instead, he raises himself as tall and fluffy as possible and exclaims "Beeeeagle."

"Fine," says Neil "Step up Big Eagle" and takes him to the couch beneath the window to bird and people watch. Pickles becomes a fierce guard dog. Neeka likes to sit on the corner of the couch and bark at anybody walking by and Pickles has taken up the cause. He sits in Neeka's spot and barks "Woof Woof Woof!" This alerts Neeka who comes to join him. The two of them stand barking their warnings to all intruders. I can only imagine what this looks like to people walking by.

Later, Pickles perches on the arm of the couch next to Neil's face and asks "Wanna snack?" Neil agrees and hands him a pine nut. "Want anudder snack?" Neil gives him another. About every 3 or 4 snacks, Pickles cranes his neck out to give and receive a kiss from daddy.

Snack time is over and Pickles asks for a "good story". Pickles places his beak against Neil's lips and says "Talk to the beak." I don't think Pickles really cares about the story, he just likes the sound and feel of the vibration against his beak. Neil's obliges while going cross-eyed trying to watch Pickles eyes for signs that Pickles is not pleased at this particular story. He's a gentle bird but only a fool would get complacent with a bird around their face. But all is well and Pickles draws bored with Neil's tale of how the chickadees like to eat Mountain Ash berries and how they eat so many that they become funny little drunken flyers.

It's almost bedtime and Pickles is getting sleepy. Neil is watching TV while lying down with his arm draped across the back of the couch, absent-mindedly scratching Pickles' neck. Pickles grabs Neil's finger to swing upside down but Neil isn't prepared. Pickles slides on his back, down the back of the couch, across Neil's chest, continuing to slide across the couch seat, landing on the floor – still on his back. He never flapped his wings or panicked, just shot from top to bottom like a sleek upside down, out-of-control little bobsled – then lay on his back on the floor with little footsies clenching and unclenching as a sign for Neil to offer him a finger to grab hold of.

I'm thinking that that will teach Pickles to hold onto us a little better but nope – once rescued and brought back to the top, hanging upside down, he let go to do it all over again. But this time he landed wedged between Neil and the back of the couch. Much to Pickle's disappointment, he was never again able to duplicate that same downhill momentum.

Now it's time for bed and after feeding Pickles his nighttime almond, Pickles climbs into his cage and into his tent. He waits for a minute or two then pokes his head out to say "Lights off!" backs up and parks himself. We turn out his light and partially cover his cage while Pickles tucks his head under his wing to dream of snacks and toys and songs and scratches to come.

It's wonderful having a parrot that likes going to bed at night. Maybe it's because he has the freedom to be out of his cage all day long, or maybe he just likes going to bed. In the summer, we always expect him to stay up as long as it's light outside, and the first couple of years he did but now, most of the time he wants to go to bed between 5:30pm and 6:30pm. We only cover him with a white sheet so it doesn't make it that dark inside of the cage and sometimes he goes right to sleep in his hanging tent but most times he just hangs out by himself, ignoring us. Earlier, he was nice about going to bed but since then, he has become more demanding. Now when Pickles takes the notion to go to bed, you'd darn well better help him out with this, or else.

The first thing he does is climb from his play stands, into his cage and on to his favorite perch. Throughout the trip he's chattering … "Bye-bye. Wanna almond snack. Lights off. Bye-bye now." From there he's happy to sit on his perch singing and talking while he waits for us to turn off his light and hand him an almond. But sometimes we get delayed, so the squawking starts. He's warning us but we're in the middle of a TV program. He scrambles out of his cage – and I'm pretty sure he's actually stomping in anger – sits on his door, yelling and flailing his wings as if to say "Hey stupid! Didn't ya here me? Turn the bloody lights out and get me my snack!" He doesn't wait for a reply, he just does an about face and heads back to his perch.

We heed his call and hop into action. We prepare his majesty's chambers while Pickles sits on his throne above us, barking orders and probably wishing he had a megaphone. I know darn well that if we were to fashion one for him, he'd know exactly how and when to use it.

Tasks are done in the order he demands. Lights off first – this is important. If you give him his almond before that, he hurls the nut to the cage floor and hollers "What are you, some kinda idiots?!" Okay, he doesn't really say that but the tone while he hollers "Lights OFF!" clearly denotes it.

So, the lights are off, Pickles has his almond in one talon and has calmed down enough to treat us with a bit of respect. "Fresh water" he politely reminds us. "Good brats" he praises.

From here, Pickles happily surveys his kingdom while chowing down on his nut. But now it's important to be at his beck and call for the moment he decides he should be covered. But we forget. Suddenly there's a screaming, flapping bird sending anything in the room that isn't nailed down into a dusty, swirling little hurricane.

97

Neil jumps into action, grabs the cover and heads for the cage while Pickles stomps back in the cage with evil backward glances. He cheers up as he sees the cover descending over him and whistles his very own, made up bedtime song - we don't know where it came from but he only sings it as he's being covered. The whole while, he's all fluffed up, standing tall as possible with splayed wings. "Good night Big Eagle" Neil says and drops the cover over the cage. But it's not the end.

We only cover the cage in the front and sides (part way down), leaving Pickles able to peer around to see us if he chooses. Once the cover is in place, we are expected to peel back one corner so he can hang on the bars for kisses and talon tickling. After a minute he gets back on the perch, fluffs up and talks himself to sleep.

One particular night doesn't end there, as it usually does. After a few minutes, there's a ruckus going on in the cage. Pickles is banging hanging toys, throwing his bucket of talon toys to the ground and raking a little metal cup across the his cage bars yelling "WANT OUT!" Okay, maybe it's not a little metal cup but something is being banged across the bars and he IS yelling "WANT OUT. WANT OUT."

We find it strange that he wants back out but we humor him by uncovering him and fastening his cage door back in the open position. Out he scrambles, hands on his hips, and begins to scream at us. Okay, he didn't have his hands on his hips but I'm sure only because that would be physically impossible for him. "Lights OFF!" he commands then runs back in his cage.

What the heck?? He wants OUR light out too?? Jeeeeeez. We cover him back up and turn off the light above us. There we sit, in the dark, pouting and wondering at what point in the last few years did we became slaves to a bird?

98

I should mention that Pickles UV light sits on the TV with a long arm that reaches to a spot right above his favorite perch. We have to reach up and hit a switch to turn it off. When Pickles wants it turned off, he stretches his whole body toward it and says, "Lights off" while making the clicking sound of the switch.

Pickles, like most parrots, is obsessed with the phone. I would buy him his own except he'd just destroy it. But wouldn't it be cool to phone him and teach him to answer and have a conversation with us? He likes to have our phone put up to his ear so he can listen to people on the other end so I can just imagine the conversations he'd have with his own telephone. I can also imagine the bill he'd rack up from dialing.

One day, I need to make a telephone call and an appointment. I settle on the couch and begin to dial the 11-digit long distance number. Pickles decides to help by making the sounds of the numbers beeping. I'm half way through and, oh crap, was that the beep of my number or his? I have long fingernails and my phone isn't nail friendly, often my nail slips off the number. Hang up, start to dial again. Oops, too many beeps, I think I missed one. Redial, faster, before Pickles can chime in. Nope, Pickles starts to dial just as fast. Several attempts later, I'm hoping I have the right number as the phone is ringing in my ear – it's long distance, after all.

Bingo, I have the receptionist on the line and we begin our conversation. Part way through, the receptionist asks what kind of dog I have. I start to wonder why she would ask that then suddenly realize Pickles is barking in the background.

"Oh" I answer, "That's just my bird."

"You have a barking bird?" she asks.

"Yes." I sigh.

Pickles switches to crow calls and begins cawing.

"Oh!" She exclaims, "You have a CROW! That's pretty cool"

"No, no, he's a parrot – an African Grey." I explain.

"Really? Does he talk too?" She asks.

"Oh God, yes." I tell her.

"Can you make him talk for me??" She asks, all excited.

"Probably." I respond and take the phone receiver over to Pickles.

"Talk to the lady Pickles." I say.

"Now?" Pickles asks.

"Yes please." Say I, "Say hello."

Pickles goes "Hoo, hoo hoo, hoo." (An owl)

"No, speak Pickles."

"Chicka dee dee dee." Goes Pickles.

"Aw, c'mon Pickles." I say.

Pickles responds with a loon call.

I glare at him; he looks innocently back at me then makes a fart sound.

Okay, that's it. I take the phone back and tell the lady that Pickles doesn't feel like talking right now.

"Hmmmm." she says, "Was that a fart I heard?"

"Yeah, he makes that sound." I admitted.

"Wonder where he learned THAT." She responds, a little snidely.

I'm thinking, listen lady, I just want to make my appointment and get the heck off this phone so I change the subject.

Finally, the receptionist is saying "Okay Mrs. Abbott, your appointment is set for Tuesday, December ..." and Pickles lets go with a loud police siren.

"No way that was your bird!" She exclaims. "How does he learn these things?"

"We live in a bad neighborhood." I lie. "See you in a couple of weeks."

As I hang up, Pickles beeps his own hanging up sound while saying 'bye-bye' and immediately begins to chat it up with actual words and phrases.

"Oh, so NOW you wanna talk."

"Now." He says, in agreement.

Cleaning time around the house is especially entertaining for Pickles. He loves to converse while we're doing housework and that's usually when we have our best conversations. It makes a chore, which I consider worse than working in the salt

101

mines, a little more bearable. All the activity, especially if both Neil and I are involved, gets Pickles quite animated. He'll yak at us while hanging upside down on a perch or boing or lie in wait for a head to absentmindedly wander close enough for a bop on the head. It provides him the chance to yell 'Score!" and have a good snicker. The best opportunities come from cleaning the cage though because it's the best place to trap a head while you perch on the cage door. If you don't get it going in, there's only one escape and it's ambushed on the way out when it's eyes are on the wrong side. It's good-natured enough but jeez, sometimes he really nails us.

The cage is the first order of business in the living room. No point cleaning a cage if you've already vacuumed because food and dried poop ends up all over the floor, especially when Pickles is helping to dispose of it by ripping the paper. Neil always announces his intentions by telling Pickles "Daddy clean the cage now" and Pickles will scramble like a spider to help, whooping it up the whole way.

We're not the most consistent housecleaners so poop sometimes accumulates on the base of Pickles' play stand. We pull out the scraper and sweep it into little piles that are as tempting as piles of leaves to children. Piles of stuff require jumping right in the middle and scattering it as fast as you can with your feet and beak.

Pickles loves the vacuum cleaner with all its noise and he competes with it to be heard. One day I pulled out the vacuum and the belt was broken so I used our tough little hand-held. I set it on the floor between Pickles at the bottom of his play stand and Neeka on the edge of the couch then went to plug it in. I returned, got on my hands and knees and turned it on. Neither of them had expected it. They both startled with a shot as one flew into the wall and the other into a window. I wasn't expecting the kerfuffle and in my shock, I knocked over my tea which startled them even further. Neeka took off running down the hall and

Pickles followed, figuring Neeka had a good escape plan, which only terrified Neeka further to have a bird fast on his tail.

I arrived in the bedroom at the end of the hall to find Neeka trapped in the corner by Pickles on the bed. I rescued Neeka by picking up Pickles and taking him to the laundry room where I was doing a load of wash. Pickles had completely regained his composure and was happy to be set down on the chest freezer while Neeka was just happy to be away from both bird and vacuum. Just then, the washing machine went into it's rinse cycle, a noisy affair from the spinning old relic, and Pickles, who'd never experienced it before, went stone still with wide eyes. I didn't want another panic on my hands so I immediately started to whoop it up, acting like it was a party with music. Pickles wasn't sure he should trust me at first but quickly realized, THIS was better than the vibrations from the freezer! The whole room shook, causing everything and everybody to convulse, and this was truly wonderful to Pickles.

I had a hard time getting him to step up off the freezer that day. Laundry had become the best household chore ever!

I have no idea why Pickles likes to be left alone but frankly, it's a little insulting. He can be miserable as hell but as soon as he knows we're leaving the house, he's happy as a lark. When we cover him up at night, as far as he's concerned, we're gone and he prefers his own company to ours so he has a great time with himself. The fun and conversations he has by himself are far better than when he's with us. Sometimes we turn off the TV to listen and we'd swear he has split personalities, just from all the sensible questions and answers.

Earlier on, we had started leaving the room when he was cranky and demanding but it's come to the point that when we do it now, we think he's done it on purpose so he can be alone! He's cranky, we say "Bye-bye cranky bird", he perks right up, says "Bye-bye. Be gone long time" and he's off somewhere to amuse himself.

103

Now we're stuck in another room with nothing to do and if we return, he gets cranky again. Sheesh.

I have to leave the house one day and give Pickles some Cheerios on the way out. He grabs one in his talon, waves it in the air and calls, "Go bye-bye" then chows down on it. In between bites, he whistles and chirps, happy to see me go. I don't put him in his cage; I just close the screen door between the living room and kitchen.

Later, when I returned home and drove into the driveway, I spotted a little grey head peeking over the top of the couch in front of the window. Or at least I thought I did, it was there then gone in a flash. I parked and stared at the window. Just as I was beginning to think I'd imagined it, up pops a head again but a split second later, it's gone again. I sat. He popped up then down again. The little jack-in-the-box antics continued several more times. Was he hiding? Did he think I couldn't see him if he was quick enough? Was this a game? He was obviously clinging to the backrest of the couch and I wondered if he was doing his usual snickering head bobs each time he ducked back down.

Eventually I went in the house but when I arrived in the living room, there was no bird on the couch. Oh great, up to his vanishing acts again. But I glanced at his cage and there he was, perched inside with one leg tucked up as if he'd been sitting there innocently the whole time.

"I saw you in the window Pickles" I accused.

"Where Daddy?" he responds, changing the subject.

"At work." I answered.

"Hasta make some money?" Pickles asked.

104

"That's right Pickles," I said as I turned to put the groceries away.

"Want some supper" Pickles called out. I told him it was too early for supper but then glanced at the clock to find it was 5:00 on the button. That bird has a built in time clock.

I brought him his supper, telling him it was a good supper tonight "It's a berry supper Pickle Boy – you're favorite birdie bread".

Pickles doesn't miss a beat, "mmmmmm! A berry good supper!" he quipped.

How clever.

Now, some readers might think that it's irresponsible of us to leave Pickles alone in the living room but you have to know Pickles, and you have to know us. Pickles' good nature stems from his sense of independence and the ability to make his own decisions. The more freedom he has, the happier he is. We could force him into his cage when we leave but it would make him angry and he'd be frustrated the whole time he was contained. Neil and I have been blessed with careers that allow us to either take him with us, work at home, or work different shifts so that Pickles is seldom left alone for long. However, sometimes circumstances change for brief periods of time and we're not home much. This would be hard for a parrot like Pickles because he's so use to company and freedom from the cage that we just can't bring ourselves to force him into it. Are there dangers associated with allowing him to stay out of his cage and alone in the living room? Of course. Pickles stays aloft 99.9 percent of the time and even when he does come to the ground or the couch, he's not comfortable there for long so he scrambles back up his cage but yes, there's a tiny chance that he might decide to explore but the house is fairly well bird proofed. Fortunately, he's not particularly destructive or much of an explorer.

105

Neil and I haven't taken a vacation in 8 years. We don't like to leave him alone for more than one night and a babysitter is out of the question because we're the only real bird people we know. I can't imagine a non-bird person trying to get along with Pickles for any amount of time BUT my mom volunteered. Stupid, stupid woman.

She's probably spent more time around Pickles than anybody else we know. She comes to stay with us for a week or two, a couple of times a year. She's fascinated with Pickles, has fun bantering with him and Pickles likes her but she never handles him - there just never seemed to be a need. Pickles isn't a warm and fuzzy bird who wants to sit on you. He'd rather sit next to you on the couch arm, or run across the back of the couch and look out the window. Sure, sometimes he gets cuddly but if someone isn't used to the way he demands to be handled, there just might be a little bit of blood.

But mom has offered. We figure there's no real need for handling, Pickles would be okay in the living room with his cage, play stand and toys. He goes to bed on his own and lets you know when to cover and lock him in. There might be the odd, startled fluttering down to the floor but if you ignore him long enough, he'll climb back up his cage. So, everything's set. Yeah, right.

The first day was fine. The minute we landed at our destination, I checked my email. Some emails were to us but sometimes it was just a 'cc' of what she was reporting to her friends - most of them are Pickles fans. Mom reports ...

"So far, the animals have survived. Pickles has asked for "snacks", "juice", "grapes", "fresh water" and at 5:00pm, "supper". He wants it at 5:00, or else. He's also asked me if I "wanna go home", "wanna party", "want some music?", "wanna sing a song, woo hoo" then informed me he'd "be right back" and marched off to the other end of his play station. About 8:00pm he told me "lights

106

off" a couple of times, as I didn't turn them off right away. After fooling around a bit with some of his musical toys, he went into his cage and climbed into his sleeping tent."

So far, so good.

As time went on, emails would pop up now and then ...

"Just in case you open any email, everything is fine. Pickles just asked me if I wanted "some breakfast cakes". It's 6:45pm and it appears that there is a major party going on and I think he may have made a few long distance phone calls while I was on the computer. Neeka is quite content. I also have not heard one word about daddy going bye-bye, be right back."

We had been afraid Pickles would whine non-stop about Daddy going bye-bye and asking if Daddy would be right back. Nice that he's not driving her crazy with that.

We had been worried that Pickles would miss us and possibly start pining. Well, apparently not ...

"Pickles is hungry today and seems to be eating everything in sight. Yesterday he just picked at his peas and I found most of his birdie bread thrown on the bottom of the cage. He ate his Pom Pom and nut with no problem and, of course, snacks. Today, he's right into everything, including his seeds. Maybe he was missing you yesterday. All that seems to have been forgotten now. He's happily chatting away. When I opened the cage this morning, he grabbed hold of the door and kept pulling it shut. Don't know if he was trying to ride out on it, or didn't want it open. Anyway, all is good."

How cute, Pickles is playing games with mom.

107

"Well, today we are apparently under attack by aliens or terrorists, I'm not sure which. Pickles has taken over the command center. I'm not sure which side he's on. There have been scud missiles (incoming and outgoing), sirens, bombs, explosions, bells ringing, water gurgling and numerous secret phone calls with muttering and a lot of 'huh?s' and "OK, bye" followed by beeps and whistles. God knows what will happen tomorrow. I'm almost afraid to go to bed in case there's a midnight attack. This is Zoe, reporting from the war zone."

He does have quite the repertoire.

"The war is over, time for celebration. After a hard day in the trenches yesterday, Pickles has called a cease-fire and is now organizing a Celebration, asking "Wanna Party? Woo hoo!" Early this morning, he informed me he was "going to go get some fresh water". Probably for the troops. Again today with the phone calls, although there was a lot of "wanna party" while making calls. I believe the menu includes (besides fresh water) juice, pom pom, grapes, potato, snacks (incidentally, snacks are only obtained after you 'poop on paper') and music. The music program includes the songs 'Banana Phone, boop boop a doop', 'Good Morning, life's sweet with orowheat' and 'Home, Home on the Range'. His list is short. Of course, anyone auditioning that doesn't measure up to his standards will be told, "Sing a GOOD song!" Talk about a tough director. I'll let you know how this all turns out. Reporting from the mess hall behind the trenches ..."

Next day. The novelty's wearing off?

"Day 5 of incarceration. Something has been going on in the cage ever since lock down and lights out. I don't know what it is and I'm sure not going to check. There have been no recognizable words so I must assume that it is all in code. I am beginning to get a little tired of "My Favorite Things", both whistled and played on his music machine, over and over and over and over. Other than that,

108

all has been clear on the Northern Front today. This is Zoe, reporting from under the bedcovers with a flashlight".

The day after …

"Pickles is starting to get frustrated with the new idiot. Pickles decided that he wanted to sleep in his log cabin on top of the cage tonight. He went in and beat up the ball that hangs on it and then was verrrrry quiet for about 45 minutes. Then he popped his head out to see if I was watching, and popped it back in for another 15 minutes. I guess he got bored then because he came out and went to bed. Silly bird. PS – It doesn't help that Pickles keeps telling Neeka that "Daddy's home".

That bird. He loves to torment the dog and in 2 years, Neeka still hasn't caught on.

"Hello. Just sat down to send you a note. I heard a noise coming from the living room but Neeka was playing with his toys so I didn't get up right away. After a minute, I turned around and guess what? There was Pickles toddling into the computer room to see what was going on. Guess he wanted to tell you "Hi". He seemed a bit put out that I would turn off his lights and then leave the room. It was like he was telling me it was bedtime because when I took him back, he went right into his cage and into his tent."

We often move Pickles from room to room for different scenery or to be with us. Mom sees us doing this all the time, but we never thought to tell her not to do it herself because she's not used to handling him and doesn't know when he might bite …

"Pickles is in the dog house. He bit me. I took him for a walk to the dining room where he has a smaller cage and he can sit on top of it and watch the "baby

109

butts", as he calls small birds such as juncos, chickadees etc. When I went to take him back, he bit me so I waited awhile and then tried to entice him with his pine nuts. When I told him to 'step up' onto my hand, he bit me and grabbed the bowl of pine nuts, which I then dropped. Now pine nuts are everywhere so I cleaned as many as I could out of the cage without him attacking me again, and swept most of them off the floor. He ate what he could find in crevasses and then proceeded to climb down to the floor for the few he could see there. I stopped that right away by yelling, "You get back up!" He scuttled up to the top of the cage and proceeded to fight with everything he could find, as well as attacking a piece of wood attached to the cage. Now that I have left the room, he is happily whistling and chatting away. I just heard some banging on the other side of the wall from where I am so went to see what's up and there's Pickles sitting calmly on the cage with his talon in the corner of his mouth like 'Mini Me'. Back to the computer and he's now whistling nonchalantly and going through every birdcall, dog bark, whistle, sneeze, sniff and phone rings and beeps. Guess he's going to be staying in there for a while. So, that's how Pickles is."

Okay, now there's blood. At least she has the presence of mind to leave the room. That's how we deal with temper tantrums. But everything continues to go downhill …

"So, at about 5:30pm, Pickles decided he would rather have snacks and supper than stay in the dining room all alone until Tuesday. The little brat. Every time I asked him if he wanted to step up, he attacked me and growled and glared at me and called me names like Rat..$%!#!$#. Now he's whistling on top of his cage in the living room … dum da dum dee dee, like nothing ever happened. Aaaaaaaaaaaaaghhhhhhhh."

He can be fierce. Later that night …

"Finally, ... the little brat has gone to bed ... in his cage ... in the living room ... in his tent. He's been pretty pleased with himself all day. I was ready to threaten him with a cooking pot but he'd have just given me the raspberry, so what's the use. The last half hour he's been happily whistling away, sitting on his cage door after asking for a grape and then throwing it at me. If he were female, I'd say he had pms. Tomorrow's another day ... whewwwww. You can just commit me when you come back.

Apparently, Pickles had stayed in the dining room for 6 hours. Mom said he was bored to tears with no food or water. She put her big fuzzy housecoat on and pulled the sleeves down over her hands and by then he really wanted to go home so he didn't make much of a fuss.

We felt pretty bad when we got back. Mom told us that it had been quite upsetting to her when Pickles wouldn't leave the dining room. All day long, she worried that he would be hungry for his supper and thirsty for water. She didn't realize we had bowl set-ups on that cage to feed him. She was convinced that she'd never get him back home and it scared her. He's had a taste of her blood and she didn't want to go near him again. She had been in tears that night.

If Pickles outlives us, we may never have another vacation again.

Chapter 8

Pickles at Eight Years of Age

I won't say living with Pickles has been easy, or that it's always fun. He demands a lot of attention and while he can sometimes be amusing when he gets in those moods, it can be exhausting trying to please him and keep him happy. We supply him with tons of toys and foraging opportunities, we spend a lot of time with him, he's free to come and go from his cage, he gets plenty of food and snacks and yet he will act like a bored child who you're at a loss to entertain. For all my complaining about him, he can be even more critical of us. Sometimes I pray his vocabulary doesn't increase because I'm afraid of the verbal abuse!

We are constantly searching our minds for new and creative ideas or items that will entertain Pickles – constantly. It's very trying but worth the effort and very rewarding to us when we succeed in anything that occupies his time and makes him happy. Our lives revolve around Pickles - it has to. A busy bird is a happy bird. I make most of his toys and in fact, it takes one small room in our house to store all his extra toys, toy parts, play stands, perch material and all his paraphernalia. His stuff occupies almost 1/2 our living room and ¼ of our dining room. Everything in the house had to be bird proofed to keep him safe and to keep him from destroying our precious belongings. He's not a particularly destructive bird but we need to err on the side of caution. Years ago, he started reprimanding himself for chewing on things he shouldn't. If he reaches for taboo items, he stops himself by saying "No! Stop it! Stop being a brat!" and when he obeys himself, he rewards himself with "Good boy. Want a scratch?"

112

Boredom can be devastating for a bird. A parrot that isn't engaging his mind, might engage in feather plucking instead. Many other things can cause plucking in a bird too and we had a bit of a scare recently when Pickles started plucking the feathers on his chest and legs. Not knowing the cause, we began to search for it by changing his diet, looking for objects in the room that might be stressing him, changing temperatures, poop inspection but we couldn't seem to find the cause. I had just decided to take him to the avian vet, which would mean a long drive and an overnight stay, when I noticed some interaction between him and Neil. Neil has a laptop and usually uses it in the dining room where he sets Pickles for company. From my computer, in a room down the hall, I can listen to the both of them talking and one day I heard Pickles doing his annoying little squeak for attention. Neil had been absorbed in something on the computer and was absentmindedly trying to appease Pickles so every time Pickles squeaked, Neil responded. After listening to this for quite some time, aware that it was getting worse, I walked in and warned Neil about what was happening. Of course, he hadn't been aware of what he was doing but agreed that he had to stop it.

I started to watch them closer. Neil was getting better at ignoring Pickles by not responding to his squeaks but now he was making the mistake of leaving the computer to give Pickles a snack or take him for a walk when he got cranky. I talked to him about that too but he said he didn't agree, that he always waited until Pickles was quiet for a few moments before he gave him attention. I watched and waited as the situation grew worse and then I noticed something else. Neil had been off work all winter with his seasonal job but now it was spring and he went back to work at the Park. I'm now working from home and alone with Pickles all day. Pickles is fine, he rarely squawks for attention and his feathers are growing back in the tiny little bald spots. They grow in but a couple of days later they're gone again. This happens over and over, and again I realize that the few hours Neil is home while Pickles is awake, he's giving Pickles attention at the wrong time and Pickles is in constant demand of attention. I mention it again to Neil and

113

after some discussion we realize Neil had been over-compensating out of guilt for not being around as much. As soon as we remedied the situation, Pickles stopped plucking completely. Since then, there have been a couple of times where Pickles will start to pluck again but we immediately realize that we've been slacking off and enabling him. Neil is the worst but I've been guilty of it too and it usually takes the other person to notice. At least we discovered the cause and thank God it's not a health issue.

Pickles is getting happier and happier about us leaving the room he is in. We're developing a bit of a complex about it and feeling a little snubbed but it's working to our advantage. Pickles has make it a common practice to turn his back on us out of disdain for our behavior but now he's snapping "Go bye-bye" and pointedly facing the other way. So now, when he gets cranky, it's easy to make him happy by telling *him* bye-bye and finding something else to do. The happy, loud animations are a sure indication that he prefers his own company to ours.

Most of the time, he's happy to entertain himself. He can talk to himself for hours and shows his amusement with head bobs and chuckles. He likes to practice his sounds and will pick up any new ones he hears in seconds. He doesn't practice his words by mumbling to himself, as many African Greys do, he just spits them out when you least expect it. He's very good at stringing whole sentences together and the longest sentence he has spoken contained 16 words, although I can't recall what he said at the time. An example of a typical shorter sentence would be "Don't you wanna eat some potato supper with your beak?" or "Let's go party in the aviary and listen to some music" or "Step up and let's go for a walk and sit on the freezer". He is perfectly capable of inserting different words into a sentence to indicate what he wants, such as telling us what he wants to eat with his beak or going for a walk to get a snack instead of going to the freezer. What he hasn't grasped yet, is that eating with 'your' beak isn't the same as eating with 'my' beak but then; we haven't really explained that to him.

114

At last count, 3 or 4 years ago, Pickles had about 100 words in his vocabulary. As he picks up new words, he will drop others. Sometimes he will drop words or phrases for months or years then suddenly decide to use them again, with a vengeance. I don't know why some words or phrases are more desirable to him than others, or why there are some things he refuses to say at all. There are many words he understands but does not repeat. If you mention a walnut he goes nuts in anticipation but he has never spoken the word.

I think the only consonant he has trouble with is 'v' but he does say 'very'. I should actually listen closer to see if he is substituting. I have a younger brother who stuttered in his early years and he would substitute consonants that he had trouble pronouncing but he'd talk so quickly that it wasn't always noticeable. In the beginning, Pickles had a bit of a problem saying anything with an 's' without whistling but now it only sounds like a lisp. And only when the 's' is at the end of a sentence, not at the beginning.

Neil and I have found that we don't always hear Pickles' new words and phrases, maybe because we don't pay enough attention or maybe because we just expect certain words to come out of his mouth. Often people will laugh about something he just said and repeat it to us and we tell them that Pickles doesn't say that particular work or phrase, that they just imagined it. But lo and behold, at some point later, we actually hear it. It was like that whenever Neil worked out of town and I was home alone with Pickles. Neil would come home and comment on new words Pickles had picked up, words I hadn't even noticed.

I'll digress for a moment about Pickles' whistling. As I mentioned, I don't whistle very well and sometimes I can't hit certain notes in a whistling song. Pickles seems to have a natural talent and an ear for music because he will learn a song that I whistle and actually insert the proper notes! I have never heard him sing off key.

115

I won't lie to you and tell you that Pickles talks coherently every day, all day long and entertains us non-stop. I started writing the PickleStories for Good Bird Magazine a few years ago and sometimes I'm worried that I won't have a story for the deadline. He does amusing things everyday but it's not always things I can put into words. Also, I prefer the stories to be somewhat of a cognitive nature and sometimes he just babbles like a toddler who's learning and practicing words. He's extremely articulate when it comes to getting what he wants and he's good at initiating conversations and following through but only when it suits him.

I wouldn't say Pickles is smarter than other parrots and I think the only reason he's so vocal is because he's so demanding. It's important for him that everybody is at his beck and call so it's to his advantage to speak well. Words work for him. Communication is important to him whereas some parrots prefer physical contact, playing or cuddling with their people or just playing on their own. Like people, all birds are individual and Pickles just happens to be a very vocally social bird with tyrannical tendencies. I mean, what is a King without a voice?!

Every PickleStory I have written has been initiated by Pickles, rather than acting on cue. We have resisted training him any tricks and the only way he increases his vocabulary is through normal conversation with him, or between Neil and I. Not to say we will never teach him tricks because it would be great interaction and a good way to keep his mind occupied.

It can be difficult to write PickleStories in the sense that I can't describe his inflections, his tones. He talks in several voices – mine, Neil's, his own and he has his happy, sad, angry, demanding voice and his very, very sweet voice. What's hard to put into words are all his antics and behavior. Most of his shenanigans don't get written about but I keep a rough diary of almost everything he does.

116

He knows how to ask for different food items or things he wants to do, such as going for a walk, going outside to the aviary, listening to music or for us to sing a song. When he asks for music, it must be his kind of music otherwise he gives you the buzzer. He knows what's scary to him and tells us with both words and actions. He only says "Good morning" in the morning and only asks for his lights off at night. At 5:00pm, on the dot, he asks for his supper. If he's somewhere he doesn't want to be, he asks to go home.

He seems to understand "Be right back". If we say it when we're leaving, it makes him happy however, if we say, "Bye-bye, be gone long time" he will often give us a little whine of disappointment – especially if it involves Daddy. If Neil's not home, Pickles will ask, "Daddy's home?" and if I respond, "He'll be right back" Pickles shows his happiness with hoots and whistles. But if I say "Daddy be gone long time" he will repeat as a question, "Gone long time?" then fluff up and pout. Pickles will often turn his back on us and scamper away saying "Bye-bye, be right back" but he never tells us "Bye-bye, be gone long time". Is it because he knows he's not going to be gone for long? Hard to say.

It's only when he's ready for bed that he'll tell us to turn his light off but he'll also use the same words a few minutes later when he's ready to be covered for the night. He might not know the difference but he's clever enough to know that both make it dark for him. He doesn't know the difference between pop and juice but he knows it's not water (he's not allowed pop). He doesn't know the difference between pudding and jello, he thinks anything served to him on a spoon is pudding but if you serve him mashed potato on a spoon he will say "mmmmm, potato". He loves peas but if he asks for a bean and you hand him a pea pod, he'll throw it in your face. If his water dish is soiled with food scraps, he'll ask for fresh water and if you don't give him fresh water with each meal, he will politely ask for it before he dines.

Pickles knows the difference between a question and a statement. Lately, he's added the "I" to things like "wanna snack" or "wanna go for a walk" but usually it's the latter. When he's demanding something he'll say, "wanna snack" but if we're busy and he's not sure if we'll give him what he wants, he'll politely ask "Wanna snack?" Same words but shows the difference between 'Can I?" and "I want."

One of the PickleStories I wrote for Good Bird Magazine makes a good example for both Pickles' understanding of teasing and what is scary. This is what I wrote …

Pickles has this thing he likes to do – pretending to fall over. He picks the thinnest branch on his play stand so that he can wrap his talons around it loosely, like little hoops, which enables him to fall upside down then flap his wings to get back up. Sometimes he just hoops his talons and flies round and round the branch. Today he is particularly animated about it.

A blood-curdling scream pierces the air and wild wing flapping sends dust and downy white feathers swirling through the room. Our living room must look like a snow globe from the street. Pickles sees he now has my attention.

"Oh no!" he exclaims. His eyes are wide and have the look of fear as he begins to fall backwards, in slow motion. He pretends to be trying to fight gravity but to no avail. He falls, clinging to the branch, upside down. "That's scary," he informs me.

"Yeah, right" I say, and go back to reading my book as he flaps his way back to the top of the perch.

Suddenly he's screaming "No, no, no, no, no!" and I look up just as he's falling backwards again. He hangs there, looking at me. "Ooops" he says.

118

Once again, he flaps to right himself on the perch then immediately goes "Ack!" and falls again. "Upside down bird" he says, "Scary."

"Pickles …" I start to say, but he interrupts with "Get back up!"

"That's just what I was going to say – get back up and stop being a little faker," I told him.

As he flapped to get back up, he flapped all the way around the branch and ended up upside down again. Flapped again, this time doing several laps around the branch but at some point he lost his grip – and it happened as he was in the upside down position, resulting in a upside down, flying bird smacking head first into the wall behind, landing in a crumpled heap on the floor.

I leapt to his rescue; sure that he must have hurt himself. By the time I got there, he was upright, beady eyes looking up at me, one talon in the air, asking to 'Step up".

As I picked him up, he quietly informed me "That's scary."

"I believe you this time Pickles".

Clearly, he was teasing me. He was *pretending* to fall over, he was *pretending* it was scary and in the end, it *was* scary which he indicated in an entirely different way than when he was teasing earlier. I send my stories out to friends through email and they send them on to friends of theirs. A friend of a friend (Eliza Firth) obviously 'got' it and wrote, *"Okay, there are other stories that are funnier, and somewhere his smart-ass remarks are more clever, but this is the best demonstration I've ever heard of that he understands language in a really subtle and nuanced way. That's scary."*

119

Those of you who are reading this, and have African Greys of your own, are probably aware of Dr. Irene Pepperberg, her African Grey named Alex and her research over the years. Until Alex's death in 2007, he demonstrated abilities that scientists thought impossible for birds. He could not only speak in context but could distinguish between colors, shapes and sizes and tell you what each item was, such as 'square, four corners, blue' and say which item was 'bigger' or 'smaller'. He could count and he could identify different materials such as paper, wool and wood etc.

Is Pickles as smart as Alex? I don't know. We don't work with him and test his intelligence however, we see amazing glimpses of cleverness each day. Once, I was humming while tidying the living room and Pickles asked, "Is that a song?"

"Sorta" I said, "It's called humming."

"What's in a song?" Pickles asked.

"Lyrics and melody" I told him.

He gave me the raspberry, as if to say he didn't believe me so I said, "Then you tell ME what's in a song".

"Music?" he asked tentatively.

"BINGO!" I said, shocked that he would come up with that.

Then, after I blurted out "Bingo" he told me "What a good song!" because we always sing "Bingo Was Her Name Oh".

While we're on the subject of songs, Pickles once asked "Wanna sing a beak?" and I told him "You can sing a song, or you can sing *with* your beak but you can't sing a beak". He responded with "That's crap".

You can see by the last exchange that he's just being silly and saying words that don't really go together but maybe he just made a mistake and meant to ask, "Wanna sing with your beak?" which is something he says all the time. Who knows? What I do know is that he doesn't always make sense. And sometimes, I think he's just screwing with me. Like the time he kept calling "Gary ... Gary ... Gaaaaarrrrryyyyyy".

"Who's Gary?" I ask

"Huh?" Pickles answers.

"I said, who's Gary?" I repeat.

"Scary?" Pickles asks

"Huh?" I ask.

"Scary" Pickles tells me.

"Is he?" I ask.

"Huh?" Pickles asks.

"You said he's scary Pickles. Is he?

"Gary?" Pickles asks.

121

"Yeah" I respond"

"Huh?" Pickles asks.

"Jeez Pickles, who the heck are you talking about?"

"Gary" He says.

"You're driving me crazy Pickles".

"Is it scary?" asks Pickles.

I guess that was Pickles' version of "Who's On First?"

If Pickles really wants something, he asks in clear and simple terms. If he's angry with you, he makes no bones about it and doesn't mince words. He'll tell you to 'stop it' and he'll call you names. If he's happy with you, he lets you know by telling you you're 'good'. They say you shouldn't anthropomorphize with parrots, that you can't apply human behavior or emotions to birds but Pickles is involved in almost every aspect of our lives, we spend almost all our time with him, and our experience is that they do have similar emotions. One day we'll write an article about it because we don't think this has been properly researched. It's obvious to us when Pickles is angry, sad, frustrated or happy. His body language, actions (and reactions afterwards) indicate that he knows what teasing is. For instance, any time you ask him what a dog says he will bark but the last time, when I asked, he cawed like a crow. I said no, asked him again and got the same response. This happened several times and each response came with head bobs and chuckles. He knew better but he was interested in our reactions. When I told him he was a goof and walked away, he barked.

When Pickles doesn't get what he wants and goes on a tirade of beating up toys and everything else in sight, you can't tell me this is not an angry response and emotion. When he hoots, hollers and whistles when you tell him you're going to get him a grape, this isn't a happy emotion? When he crouches, splays his wings, chews his toenail and does circles on his perch when you refuse to give him a snack, he's not frustrated? Or if he puffs up his cheeks and settles into a fluffy little ball when you deny his request to go for a walk, he's not disappointed and sad? I'm sure the scientists would debate this but when you spend as much time with a parrot as we do, it simply doesn't make sense.

Body language is not only key to understanding a parrot, but it's crucial. Anybody who says their bird never gave any sort of sign that he was going to bite isn't paying close enough attention. It can be their stance, feathers ruffling or sleeking against the body, a head movement or something as subtle as a slight change in their eyes. Parrots don't want to bite, their first instinct is to flee but that's not always possible for a domestic bird (especially one that doesn't fly) so if you don't heed their warnings, their only option is to bite. Through body language, just as they do in the wild with other birds, they are telling you what they want or don't want and if you are unable or unwilling to respect their feelings, you will pay for it.

In the beginning, Neil had a hard time learning Pickles' body language and he paid for it in blood. I remember one evening, during the previously mentioned difficult period between Neil and Pickles, when Neil was sitting on the couch with Pickles next to him on the couch arm. Pickles put his head down, bared his neck and asked for a scratch. Neil reached his finger out slowly and hesitated just before contact. Pickles whipped his head around and bit. "You pissed him off" I said, "Don't hesitate otherwise he thinks you're teasing him". Neil said he was scared because he always gets bit and I told him it's because you can't read him. I said there are times when Pickles will put his head down for a scratch just to draw you in for a bite but there are times he really wants to be scratched. His body language

123

will tell you what he's opting for. That time, Pickles wanted a scratch but was frustrated with your response because he too can read body language and he's irked that you're afraid of him, that you're such a wimp and not giving him what he wants.

A little while later, Pickles asked again for a scratch. I told Neil to pay attention to his body language and that Pickles honestly wanted a scratch. I told him not to hesitate, just do it. It took courage but Neil went in for the scratch and was rewarded with several minutes of gentle bonding. It took some trial and error for a couple of days but Neil quickly learned to read Pickles and the biting stopped.

Parrots understand body language, both with their own kind and with us. It comes naturally to them, they were born with that instinct. They can read your mood and they will behave accordingly. He's very sensitive and respectful of us when we're dead tired, or not feeling well. If we're extremely tired, he will entertain himself and if we're sick and sleeping on the couch, he's quiet as a mouse.

I've read that African Greys have psychic abilities and have had occasion to wonder about that myself. One evening, during the time Neil was working in Vancouver, he was driving home for the weekend and was expected around 8:00 that evening. 45 minutes before his arrival, Pickles suddenly went berserk and started yelling "Daddy's home! Daddy's home" but when I looked outside, there was no car. Pickles settled down after a couple of minutes and was quiet until Neil drove up 45 minutes later. The next day, Neil was telling me how good he feels coming home and that whenever he gets to the town of Merritt (45 minutes from here) he gets excited and starts talking out loud. Part of that involves saying "Pickle Boy! Daddy's coming home! Woo hoo!" and I thought, no frickin' way. But yes, Pickles was acting up and positive that daddy was home at the exact time that Neil would have been talking out loud in the car. We live a few blocks from the fire/ambulance station and I can't explain why 5 seconds before the sirens start

124

blaring, Pickles does his own siren although I suspect he hears something that we can't hear beforehand – like maybe the garage door opening.

Parrot diet is very complicated. Contrary to popular belief, Polly doesn't want crackers. Crackers are loaded with fat, salt, and trans fats. They need fresh fruit, vegetables, grains and all the right proteins, nutrients and vitamins. They can be fussy eaters so it's not always easy to maintain a healthy diet for them. 8 years later, I'm still studying everything I can get my hands on in regards to diet. I think we've done a pretty good job in providing Pickles the proper nutrition but I'll admit there are the odd times when Pickles gets a bit of crap. Once in a blue moon he gets a piece of my low-salt, low-fat potato chip, about the size of a quarter. (I should mention that Neil and I are on very low fat and salt diets.) Neil has become an expert at cooking healthy meals and even baking breads, cookies and cakes that have basically no fat. Delicious too! And sometimes Neil makes pizza so Pickles gets a tiny bit of crust. It's rare but sometimes Pickles will also get the odd piece of hard cheese, a mouthful of pudding or jello and his favorite – half a jellybean.

Neeka is also on a very good diet. We buy good dry dog food and treats, I bake most of his dog cookies and that's all he's allowed. We've never fed him people food so he doesn't ask for it. He will sleep or play the whole time we are dining or snacking and never looks at us in expectation. Every couple of months, I will sneak a little gravy, meat and potato into a dish when he's not looking and just leave it there for him to discover. That way, he doesn't know where it came from, he thinks it just magically appeared! From the moment we brought him home at 8 weeks of age, we have free-fed him dry dog food. No can food. Our vet can't get over how slim and healthy he is since Min Pins are prone to obesity, and his teeth are perfect because of the dry food, treats, rawhides and odd meat bone.

Okay, so some of you might be getting a little bored of reading stuff like this so I'll throw a little story in to break it up … I left Pickles a little too long in the

125

dining room while I worked on the computer in the room down the hall. I can tell he's getting bored with the 'baby butt birdies' outside the window but he's still calling good naturedly, "Anybody home? Hello? Wanna go to the freezer". He's being a good boy so I drop what I'm doing, pick him up and take him to play on the chest freezer in the laundry room. He runs around for a while then settles into a fluff ball, allowing the freezer vibrations to course through his body. This makes him sleepy, at least I *think* that's what's it's doing, if you know what I mean. So while he's in this content mood, I take him home to his cage in the living room and go back to the computer.

A few minutes later I hear him yelling, "Said be right backarack, jackarack!" I remembered I did tell him I'd be right back and then I forgot, but wait! Did he say 'jackarack'? He got 'be right backarack' from Neil but where the heck did the last part come from? Regardless, I headed back and shared a banana with him. He only eats the outside, leaving me with the crappy core, and the stringy stuff is flown in my face. When we're finished, Pickles indicates he wants to go back to the dining room and "listen to some music" this time, so I transport him back there and put some flute music on the CD player for him. The dining room is where we keep the stereo.

Later, while working on the computer, I'm vaguely aware of clicking on the hall floor but assume it's just Neeka. I ignore it until I hear a tiny voice saying "Let's go home" and turn to see Neeka on one side of a stuffed toy and Pickles on the other through the doorway. Neeka's looking horrified because he's afraid Pickles is after him but also because he wants the stuffed toy in front of Pickles – he doesn't like to share. But Pickles, on the other hand, is horrified by the toy and just wants to get past it and go through the doorway to get to me. "Stop it!" he yells at the toy as he paces back and forth.

It's obvious Pickles isn't very comfortable on the floor and he kinda wants to go home but he had braved the whole trek all the way to see me and wasn't comfortable about turning around to go all the way back. He wanted me to pick him up and take him home, or he wanted to join me at the computer. Meanwhile, I just sat quietly and watched the show.

Neeka and Pickles are at a stale mate. It's stressing Neeka out but it's really pissing Pickles off and Pickles takes to growling at the toy and telling it off. "Ratty beak! Stop it! Go home!" he snarls.

Neeka creeps ever so slowly up to the stuffed toy, takes a toe gingerly in his mouth and drags it carefully backwards down the hall and out of my vision. Pickles dashes through the doorway but Neeka must have thought Pickles was taking a run at him because I heard a scrambling series of clicks beating it further down the hall.

Pickles makes it to my feet and roosts there with one foot in the air, signaling that he wants up. He sits on my knee muttering over his ordeal while I surf the net looking for more stuffed toys.

Now back to the boring stuff. Flighted or non-flighted – that is the question. We've basically left that up to Pickles. He's not clipped at present and doesn't seem to take any interest in flying except when startled. He knows he can fly, and fly well. As a baby, Thomas & Sylvia allowed him to fledge before he was clipped for me. This is important as it teaches them good balance and confidence. When Pickles does fly, he can grasp my upheld finger and land with perfect grace. He can hover, mid-air until he decides which direction to go and he can bank and angle artfully. If he's startled to the floor, he's capable of flying back up to his cage but he chooses to walk and climb. After a few incidents, he seems to be learning about windows but now and then he presses his luck with softer hits.

Sometimes we feel we need to clip him, like when we go camping or stay in a cabin because his set-up is different and we don't want him startled through an

127

open door. Plus, something could happen during transportation – a cage door gets loose, a car accident or something unexpected. When we do clip him, we have to warn him that he can no longer fly. We'll hold him up over the bed and release him so that he flops onto something soft and after a couple of times, he gets it. The first time we clipped him, we were staying at a friend's place and he was startled from his cage and fell like a rock onto the porcelain tile. When he landed, he sat perfectly still and went "Uh oh." It wasn't until later that I noticed every time I gave him a snack, he dropped it. I inspected his beak and he had broken the tip off. Poor thing couldn't eat much more than mash potatoes and oatmeal for a couple of days.

Parrot behavior is an on-going research project for us. Their behavior is so very complicated and it's only recently that information on African Greys has been available because they are so close to the wild. They haven't been domesticated as long as other parrot species so they haven't been studied as much. Then there's all the 'junk' information out there, advice you want to completely avoid if you want a well-balanced, healthy bird.

African Greys, some people say, can live up to 75 years or more. This is unlikely in captivity though because, being so close to the wild, they haven't had a chance to build up immunities to certain toxins and bacteria. Regardless, they can live a long time and Pickles will probably outlive us. This is where it becomes difficult for us. A parrot owner needs to make arrangements for their parrot before they die. We have yet to find a home suitable for Pickles. It can't be just anybody; they need parrot experience, patience, preferably no children and a situation that allows Pickles the freedom he's always enjoyed. Even if we found such a place, what guarantee do we have that someone won't run into circumstances that force them to give him up? There are horror stories out there about parrots going from home to home being neglected, abused, left covered all the time or basically abandoned in a garage to go insane.

Pickles is a pretty easygoing, well-balanced bird but he expects to be treated a certain way. If he were to be put in a home where he was denied that treatment, he wouldn't be an easy bird to live with. He could end up a miserable, screaming, biting bird and who wants that? So it's on to the next crappy home who decides they want a really cool parrot but are completely unprepared and unequipped to deal with him.

As Pickles ages, he becomes more sedentary. He's not as active with his toys or as demanding of our time. He's perfectly content to sit in one spot for long periods of time, preening, napping, observing or chatting to himself. He's 8 years old now and the changes are significant. We suspected that he would get like that over time but didn't expect it at this age. Perhaps it's because Neil and I are getting older and less active and Pickles picks up on that, or maybe we're doing right by him and have shaped him into a well-balanced, content bird.

To live with an animal who can speak and communicate is truly astonishing. They have such human-like qualities but not so much that they lose their animal attraction. Let's face it; we keep animals because they're so *un*human-like. Would you like your dog or cat as much if they could speak? An animal that doesn't talk, is an escape from the human frustration we deal with every day. But then, along comes a parrot. Even if they don't speak, they are so un-like any other domesticated pet but the fact that they do, makes them so very intriguing. That a creature so small can be so intellectually engaging while melting your heart with love and affection is beyond words for anyone who's never experienced it. Pickles' intelligence challenges us to be smarter, more patient, kinder, less selfish and more humble. His playful impishness keeps us young and his happiness is contagious. Sure, he can be a cruel tyrant but with a soft, gentle side. Please The King and you will receive your just rewards and his undying loyalty.

Pickles' love is *not* unconditional. His conditions are; feed me, entertain me, be patient with me, allow me to make my own decisions, allow me my independence and to feel a sense of control over my own life, trust me, respect me and love *me* unconditionally.

We wouldn't have it any other way.

About the Author

Georgi Abbott lives in Logan Lake, British Columbia, Canada with her husband, Neil, their Congo African Grey Parrot, Pickles and their 6-pound Miniature Pinscher, Neeka.

Pickles, at 3 months of age, took over their lives in 2002. This sassy, demanding, fun loving and much too intelligent bundle of feathers occupied almost every minute of their every day lives from then on.

Georgi has been writing humorous stories about Pickles for Good Bird Magazine for several years and Pickles fans, from around the globe, have been following them through both their stories and Pickles TheParrot Face Book page.

Other books by Georgi Abbot, at this time, include, Pickles The Parrot Returns and Pickles the Parrot Speaks. Look for a 4th book in Spring, 2013.

Pickles' website: www.picklestheparrot.com
Pickles' Facebook page: http://www.facebook.com/pickles.theparrot?v=wall
Also, check out Pickles The Parrot videos on Youtube.

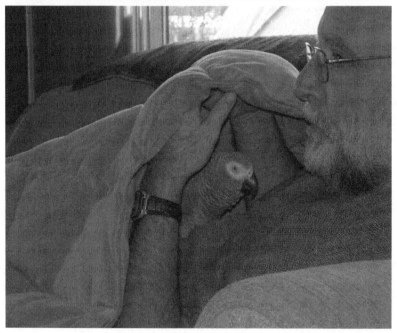